A Fellowship of Cracked Pots

William Gaskill

A Fellowship of Cracked Pots
ISBN: Softcover 978-1-946478-24-5
Copyright © 2017 by William Gaskill

All rights reserved. No part of this book may be reproduced or transmitted in any form or by any means, electronic or mechanical, including photocopying, recording, or by any information storage and retrieval system, without permission in writing from the publisher.

To order additional copies of this book, contact:

Parson's Porch Books
1-423-475-7308
www.parsonsporch.com

Parson's Porch Books is an imprint of **Parson's Porch & Book Publishers** in Cleveland, Tennessee, which has double focus. We focus on the needs of creative writers who need a professional publisher to get their work to market, **&** we also focus on the needs of others by sharing our profits with those who struggle in poverty to meet their basic needs of food, clothing, shelter and safety.

A Fellowship of Cracked Pots

Contents

A Crucial Absence 7

A Fellowship of Cracked Pots 13

All Wet and All In 20

All Wet and All Set 27

And the Winner Is 34

Big Things from Small Beginnings 40

Coffee and the Paper Are Not Enough 47

Coming, Going, Coming Again 53

Creative Crying 58

Crumb Dog Millionaire 64

Demons in Worship 70

Driving with No Brakes and No Reverse 77

Endurance 83

Funeral Wrecker 89

Get Your Ears On 96

Hearts and Treasures 102

Help for Hoarders 109

Jesus Behind Closed Doors 115

Keep on Keeping On 122

More Than We Can Bear No More 129

Naked and Unafraid 136

Particle and Wave 143

Strange Inheritance 149

The Night Time Is the Right Time 155

The Poor Man Has a Name 161

A Crucial Absence

Mark 6:34 says, "When Jesus went ashore, he saw a great crowd, and he had compassion for them, because they were like sheep without a shepherd; and he began to teach them many things."

We've learned by now that we don't have to go very far away to find the mission field. Our youth will leave in just a few minutes to go to Wilmington, Delaware and work for the week with Urban Promise. They could just as well have simply crossed route 130 and worked in Camden, or maybe stayed home and found great human need right next door or just around the corner from their house.

I'm in no way a doomsday preacher. I still find so much that is beautiful and good, so much excellence, and so many things worthy of praise to focus on. I don't want to fill my mouth with the language of atheists who see nothing but distress and evil. How shall we live a grateful, faith-filled, trusting of God's goodness life if all we ever do is carp about what's wrong? But in all honesty, I do have my moments when I think the moral and spiritual life of our land is unraveling at an alarming pace. I still see the withering effects of poverty, unemployment, and ignorance all around. I am well versed on the bitterness that is spawned by bigotry and corruption.

I'm no better than many of you in my struggle with cynicism either. I still see relationships falling apart, covenant promises routinely broken, and children abandoned, being left alone to fend for themselves and to try to figure life out on their own without wise adults to guide them. I don't have to catalogue this for you. You can watch the inventory being taken every night on the news if you want to. I'm not a political preacher because I assume you don't need me to point out all these things and more besides. Suffice it to say that in assessing the state of our world the simile, "like sheep without a shepherd" seems keenly appropriate to our day in time.

One of the earliest appearances of the simile, "like sheep without a shepherd," appears in the Book of Numbers. It's in a story at the end of Moses' life. It's a story about leadership. It's a shepherd story. God had just informed Moses, the shepherd become leader, that he was not going into the land of promise because, quote: "you did not show my holiness before their eyes at the waters of Meribah." How could Moses, who spoke with God, face to face, as a man speaks with a friend, have made such a mistake? It was probably because he was tired and fed up with all the murmuring sheep around him. Perhaps he'd had one sheep bite too many.

Moses had been surrounded by doomsday preachers, by people who complained about everything, about the food, about the lack of water, about Moses as a leader, even about God. Moses did his best to keep everyone happy and we all know that's a fool's errand. God told him how to give the thirsty tribes a long, cool drink by striking a rock with his staff, the symbol of his God appointed authority. He did as he was told and sure enough, out gushed drinking water from that least likely of all sources, from a rock.

The outcome was satisfying to the people at least until the next complaint fiesta was scheduled, but the way Moses announced the coming miracle was the problem. Moses marched to the podium that day with Aaron his brother at his side and shouted, "Ho, you rebels! Do you want us to bring forth water from this rock?" It was as though Moses stole a little piece of glory for himself that day. It was the kind of failure of leadership which God never will sanction. God does not share his glory.

God gives us much latitude in many things but God seems to be a stickler when it comes to God's glory. That's why the Bible warns us that God resists the proud and gives grace to the humble. The promises of God are promises of God alone, not God plus Moses, plus Aaron, or plus anyone else, even you and me. But God does employ human leaders to work those promises out in the world. Moses knew that much here at the end of his life and ministry.

He also knew that without godly leadership, the people would be scattered like sheep without a shepherd. They wouldn't stay together. They would lose their focus. They would split up and become prey to all sorts of predators. Their complaints would once again devour their peace and send them spinning off in all sorts of directions, looking for what their souls craved but never finding it. They would suffer hunger and thirst and die in the wilderness. Without someone to take them in, they would never enter the Promised Land, the land of God's promises. Everyone would begin more and more to do what was right in their own eyes.

Godly leadership can be hard to find. Moses recommended Joshua to God as his successor, a leader who focused not so much on the giants who always lurk around the promises of God to discourage anyone from actually taking possession of them, but a leader who will dare to believe that the promises of God are for God's people to possess and enjoy. They know the abundance that comes from walking with God.

Such leadership is what is needed in every age. As you consider your own outlook on life, are you obsessed with the giants that threaten to block your way or are you cultivating the consciousness of living in God's favor? It's easy to get lost and wander off, like a sheep without a shepherd. It's easy to lose sight of God's promises and begin to fill your head and your heart and your mouth with nothing but bad news.

Failed leadership is one thing; corrupt leadership is another. In Ezekiel 34, the prophet of God excoriates the priests of his day. They are indicted for feeding themselves but not feeding the sheep. In this period in Israel, the very people who were entrusted to present God to the people and the people to God had degenerated into simply using religion to make themselves comfortable and fat while everyone else struggled under burdens hard to bear. God said, "I will rescue my sheep from their mouth so that they may not be food for them."

Then in verses 11-16, God described what he would do for his sheep. He would seek them out, rescue them from places to which they had been scattered, gather them and bring them into their own land. He would feed them with good pasture and they would lie down in good grazing land. I myself will shepherd my sheep. I will seek the lost and bring back the strayed. I will bind up the injured and strengthen the weak, but the fat and the strong I will destroy; I will feed them with justice.

In the absence of God appointed, wise, and Spirit-filled leaders, people tend to fill the vacuum with counterfeits. In Zechariah 10:2 we read this: "For the teraphim [household gods] utter nonsense, and the diviners see lies; the dreamers tell false dreams, and give empty consolation. Therefore, the people wander like sheep; they suffer for lack of a shepherd." It all sounds so spiritual but underneath it is empty.

We live in such an age where it is in vogue to be "spiritual" but not religious. I met quite a few pilgrims on the Camino who were fond of that phrase. But the phrase is often a signifier for a spirituality that is a mile wide and an inch deep. That's why Paul cautions us to test the spirits to see if they be from God because even Satan comes disguised as an angel of light. Only God is the true light. There are many posers and many imposters.

A Fellowship of Cracked Pots

There are a few other stories in the Old Testament that use the phrase, "like sheep without a shepherd." Often the phrase shows up to describe the after effects of a military defeat. Mark is summoning them all to the surface as he gives account of Jesus' reaction to the crowds that flocked to him that day. They had physical hunger, so Jesus fed them, all 5000 of them. They had needs for healing and Jesus healed all who were brought to him. They had been spiritually misdirected, so Jesus taught them many things which would free them from dead tradition and bring them back into a living hope. Their human leaders had failed them miserably. It was and is a situation unacceptable to God.

When people want to follow God but are defrauded and deceived, God will act to correct it. We are his people and the sheep of his pasture says Psalm 100. The Lord is my shepherd says Psalm 23. We shall not want. God cares for his sheep and God summons us to faithfully be part of God's compassionate ministry.

When Mark and I were in Pamplona where they have the annual festival of the running of the bulls, we ate dinner at the Café Aruna where Earnest Hemingway was said to have hung out. There was a large outdoor café and a very ornate interior. With that memory of hanging out where my buddy Earnest hung out, I checked out his novel of the Spanish revolution, For Whom the Bell Tolls, out of the Cherry Hill library last week. The title is taken from lines of a poem by John Donne which says this:

"No man is an island, entire of its self; every man is a piece of the Continent, a part of the main; if a clod be washed away by the sea, Europe is the less, ...any man's death diminishes me, because I am involved in mankind; and therefore, never send to know for whom the bell tolls; it tolls for thee."

I close with you, our youth, especially in mind. You yourselves may have had some experience already of not having the kind of leadership you need and deserve. God has not forgotten you. The cries of your heart have not fallen on deaf ears. God hears and God cares. So now you will go into a situation where you will meet some lambs who perhaps have inadequate shepherding at home or in the city or in their school, wherever. And each one is precious. And each one is part of you. We are all connected in some way. Just as a continent can be diminished by tossing one stone from its land into the sea, so can something important begin by the placing of one small stone where God wants it to go. Trust God with the little God puts before you this week. You never know what may come.

You may have had, or someday you may have, occasion to ride the subways in New York City. When they were digging the tunnels, they needed someplace to unload the debris. They began to load it on boats and take the dirt and granite out into the harbor and dump it. Load after load after load went off Manhattan Island until a new island was born, Ellis Island. And Ellis Island became the gateway to the land of liberty and of opportunity for thousands and thousands of immigrants and refugees fleeing from the oppression in Europe and other places. What boat captain in the early days of transporting those loads of stone would have thought they were building a bridge to freedom for so many?

I believe what you are about to do in Wilmington, or maybe later in your own family, or neighborhood, or in your school has tremendous significance in the plan of God. So be diligent and pay attention. You just might find the eyes of your Good Shepherd looking upon you with love and approval.

A Fellowship of Cracked Pots

Does it ever strike you as remarkable that the fanatical Jewish fundamentalist, Saul of Tarsus, who acted more like a terrorist than a guardian of orthodoxy, was converted by the kindness and grace of God to become Paul the Apostle who planted churches all over Asia Minor and wrote two thirds of the New Testament? It would be sort of like if Osama bin Laden had had a born again experience and became the head of the Billy Graham Evangelistic Association. People back then had trouble believing that Saul's conversion was legitimate. Can we trust him? Is Saul just faking it to gain an advantage? Is his conversion real?

Beyond that, what about justice? What about all the suffering he caused? How could God just seem to let him off the hook? Is God's mercy and grace really that extravagant? Is it even right? Put yourself in the early Christian's shoes. Don't you think we'd have been scandalized if Osama got born again and wanted us all to believe it and accept the new him? Most of us were glad when we heard he'd been shot dead.

Somewhere late in the last century, evangelism became a dirty word. Sophisticated people didn't like evangelists. They seemed intellectually challenged and emotionally manipulative. When I did my Dr. of Ministry degree, it was offered by Columbia Theological Seminary with the emphasis on evangelism. Other Presbyterian schools refused to offer such a course load, merely shaking their heads and clucking their tongues. The word evangelism and the practice of evangelism had evidently fallen beneath the worthiness line of the mainline.

And so, the church growth movement was born to take the place of evangelism. Churches and denominations began to shrink at an alarming rate, a phenomenon that continues to this day. Something had to be done. So there arose the craze to make the church user friendly. Evangelism calling for a personal commitment to Jesus Christ was replaced by consumerist religion. Come be with us. We have everything you want and need. We have all the bells and whistles. We will entertain you, refresh you at our coffee bar, and give you what you so richly deserve. Welcome to the religious mall of America. We offer a veritable smorgasbord of religious products to suit all tastes.

Last Sunday, I was on vacation. True confession of your pastor: I didn't attend worship at another church. I spent Sunday morning along with the rest of the church avoidant populace. I went out on an errand. There, walking in my neighborhood were numerous people out enjoying the beautiful morning. There were joggers, dog walkers, people on bicycles, husbands and wives, fathers and daughters, pairs of women yakking, and of course the chronically connected cell-phoners with their electronic umbilical cords attached to their ear drums. They all seemed like decent, polite, middleclass people. A good time seemed to be being had by all. They probably harbored their small sins and bad habits. None I would wager were out to terrorize anyone. It would have been hypocritical of me to shout out the window, "Get to church why don't you."

I drove by the Lutheran church at Chapel Avenue and King's Highway. It was 9:35 AM. The sign said, "Services at 9:30 and 11 AM.; come join us." There was one car in the large parking lot. Did it belong to the loneliest preacher in the world, or was it the security guard's car, there to make sure no one got in? Were they closed for Labor Day? Were they closed forever? What the devil was going on there?

A Fellowship of Cracked Pots

What should those of us who habitually attend worship say to or about these growing numbers of people who are in the habit of ignoring us? In the old days, the church insiders would probably have described them as "the lost." The church growth people were smart enough to realize that calling somebody lost seemed more like a judgmental insult than an invitation to being a found person, meaning someone who attends church and gives generously to the offering so that other lost people can be found. You can rename evangelism as church growth, but what do you call the people you are trying to reach so that growth will happen? The semantic problem is thorny.

Long gone are the days of the heathen, the unregenerate, the reprobate, or the damned. We tried, "un-churched," separating outsiders from insiders. Nope; too judgmental, as though something serious is lacking in these people who don't attend. Then came the, "pre-churched" as though everyone was on the way to worship, whether they knew it or not, which at any rate is not a valid assumption. Finally, the sociologists of religion came up with the category, religious "nones"; what religion are you, Catholic, Protestant, Jewish, Muslim, Buddhist, Hindu, or none; check one. The fastest growing group in America is the religious "nones". It gets either too confusing or too depressing after a while.

Maybe we need to double back and use the term Jesus used in his two parables he told in response to the Pharisees and the scribes, representatives of the religiously serious and the biblical literalists of his day who were offended in him because, "This man receives sinners and eats with them." Jesus spoke of lost things, a shepherd's one in a hundred lost sheep and a widow's "one in ten" lost coin.

What does it mean to be lost? Let's look at them in turn, first the sheep, then the coin. I find it interesting that even people who don't go to church love Psalm 23, which as you know begins, "The Lord is my shepherd." It's an ironic text because almost no one wants to be a sheep. Sheep are notoriously helpless, depending on the shepherd for the most intensive of care and supervision. They need guidance in order to eat, where to drink, where to walk, and where to sleep. They need ideal conditions in which to thrive.

Sheep are prone to wander off even though they are essentially flock members. Sheep need to stay together, but they get so preoccupied following their appetites that they are apt to go astray. Sooner or later they, alone, fall prey to some predator, or get tangled in a thicket of briars and thorns or fall into a pit. A lost sheep has strayed from its rightful place and has separated itself from the one entrusted with its well-being. The lost sheep doesn't know how to get home from here. It needs the shepherd to come looking, to find it, and to carry it home.

Much is made about our search for God, which usually means we are looking for a deity that we prefer, that won't demand much, and won't insist on being involved in the day to day of our lives. We just want a god we can summon when the going gets rough and whom we can ignore when things go well. Christian faith speaks of a God who comes searching for us and when it occurs to us that we have been found, expects a new relationship to develop between us, one that involves sticking together through thick and thin, and one that is important to us every hour of every day, not just for one hour on Sunday. A favorite hymn of church goers and non-attendees is Amazing Grace which says, "I once was lost but now I'm found; was blind but now I see." Maybe we don't like the lost part, but maybe something deep inside us knows in spite of our pride the theological truth of what has been set to music. We all begin our journey with God as lost people.

Jesus said there is great joy in heaven when the one lost turns and begins to live into the wealth and will of God. This is called repentance. It is like when beloved family member who has wandered away into danger has come to safety. It is like we all are more complete because one who was always supposed to be with us but was separated somehow has been restored. The reunion makes heaven and earth rejoice.

It is no insult to say to someone, you are highly valuable; you are worth it. We'd like to spend time with you. We'd like to be together and we are enriched by your presence among us. We want the best for you. We want you to be safe and satisfied. We want you to be everything which God your creator intended when God created you. Which means, that we, like Jesus, need to be able to see the intrinsic worth of people. The religious only saw what was wrong with the people Jesus had dinner with; Jesus saw what was possible for people to become when they were received as friends and when that uniquely intimate of human activities occurred, sitting down and sharing a meal together.

And notice the ratio involved: just one out of a hundred was worth the search. The shepherd could have said, "I still have 99 sheep; what's one more or less?" To Jesus every single person is valuable. Every single person is worth the effort, the search, and the sacrifice. He laid down his life for sinners. Ninety nine percent of the people were already home, were already made worthy. The Good Shepherd was focused on the one percent still absent, still lost, still away, caught in snares, vulnerable to destruction, unable to find their way home. So, he searched and is searching still.

Jesus underscored his value system with the math in the parable of the lost coin. For the woman, to have nine left out of ten was not the issue. Without the one lost, she was one coin poorer. One tenth of her wealth was no trivial matter. So, she searched diligently until she found the one lost. Then it was party time. In heaven, every single person is of extreme value. Whether it is one one-hundredth or one tenth that is lost, the search is on. And God does the searching. And God invites us to be part of the search party. And it may begin with a dinner party, or some other way we discover to receive sinners and begin to treat them like long lost relatives. Whether you call it evangelism or a strategy for church growth doesn't really matter. What matters is the fact that every single person is a priority concern for God.

Maybe the church needs to stop being a self-satisfied club for the like- minded and become a rallying point for search parties. Maybe the kind of kindness and grace shown to Saul will become the kind of magnetic force that will redirect a life or two and become a great source of heavenly rejoicing.

Most of us have been watching the weather recently to see what track the hurricane Hermine would take. Dour forecasts for the Jersey shore were paraded across the TV screens. If the track veered one way, the damage would be worse than hurricane Sandy in our shore communities. The weather people showed us their spaghetti charts which illustrated all the possible options of the route the storm might travel. Low and behold, by Labor Day morning, the storm began to pull away from the coast. The imagined forecast for the worst became a much more optimistic projection, even better than predicted or hoped for. There was great joy because the storm changed direction. Wreckage was averted.

That, said Jesus, is what happens when a lost person is found and they change course. Repentance means going another direction, and to go in the direction of Jesus is to choose abundant life. And it is to choose for the Body of Christ and the worship of the living

God. Amazing Grace! You and I are called to be a part of it all through our Lord Jesus Christ.

All Wet and All In

Let me ask you to use your imagination for a minute. Imagine it is Saturday morning and I call you up. I've developed a bad case of the flu and won't be able to preach on Sunday. I say, "I'm sorry to call you at the last minute but I really am very sick. I've been noticing your growth in the Lord. You have become much more confident. You've been stepping up in leadership positions and really carrying the load. And you are a veteran of worship design teams. Some of the prayers you have written for public worship have been nothing short of inspired. Now I need to ask you a big favor. I need you to preach tomorrow. It is Baptism of the Lord Sunday and since I just baptized several of your children a few weeks ago and you came to the meeting where I explained the meaning of baptism, I thought of you. You don't have to make it real long. Everyone will be rooting for you and admiring your courage. Will you do it?"

Because of my expert skill in softening you up with flattery, meant with all sincerity of course, and because you have always said, "Pastor, if there's anything I can ever do to help you out, please let me know," you agree with great trepidation to give it a try. With great earnestness, you set your mind to the task and come up with a passable sermon. At least you won't embarrass yourself and who knows, people might actually get something out of it. No, by golly, it is really a very good sermon. You arrive here on Sunday early to pray and get settled in. Finally, it's time. Just as Earl is playing the prelude, after all those centuries of invisibility, in walks the risen Jesus Christ and takes a seat right down front. He seems delighted to be here and eager to hear what you have to say.

Now here is a little multiple choice quiz for you. Your response is:

a. You fall on your face as though dead; there is good biblical precedent for that. It's going to take angel ministry to get you back on your feet.
b. You lose consciousness altogether and faint.
c. You try to give the pulpit to Jesus. After all, he should be the one to preach, not you.
d. You rip up your sermon, flop to the floor, and like Job cry out, "I have written of things too lofty for me. I repent in dust and ashes."
e. You trust Jesus' warm affirmation and go ahead and preach your sermon. After all, you did pray as you prepared and maybe it would be disrespectful to treat what seemed like a gift from God when Jesus was invisible as something vile and unacceptable when he appeared.

How do you think John the Baptist felt that day, standing there in the Jordan River, seeing Jesus breaking the brow of the hill and striding toward him? You might say, "Yes, but for John it was different." He was appointed to his ministry from before he was even conceived by Zechariah and Elizabeth. We don't know how much they told him while he was growing up. Did they let him in on the story of his dad's angelic visitation? Had he heard of the long months of mute silence his father endured for questioning the veracity of the great angel Gabriel? What did he make of the fact that his parents were well beyond the season of child conceiving let alone parenting when he was born?

We're not told what led him to develop such contempt for the religious establishment, the brood of vipers as he called them, and head on down to the wilderness to ply his ministry in austere conditions. How did he become the intense wild man, the voice crying in the wilderness and thundering in the spiritual darkness?

You might think that all that went before would have made it easier for John than for people like you and me who are simply surprised by Jesus' presence in the midst of our everyday lives, our callings if you will. But I'm not so sure. To have your whole life shaped by an event that is coming, you know not when, only that sometime during your life, something momentous will occur, or more accurately, that someone with a much greater call and anointing on his life than you have on yours will one day show up and involve you, well, it's way beyond mind-blowing. For John that day was the day. He opted for option "c" on the multiple-choice list: "You take over from here Jesus. You are much greater than me."

At this point, grace comes fully into view. Jesus confirms the ministry of his cousin John. He calls it the fulfilling of all righteousness. The fulfillment of all righteousness enfolds several dimensions of God's grace in one moment of time. Let's unpack it a little.

First, let's consider why people were making the trip out to see John. There were no buses, trains, or cabs. They had to walk it from Jerusalem through the harsh wilderness, down the risky Jericho road, which was rife with brigands and thieves. And why did they expose themselves to hardship and danger? They came out because their souls and spirits were hungry and thirsty for righteousness. The religious establishment that ran the temple had become a brood of vipers. Jesus later in great anger accused them of turning the central place of Israel's worship into a den of thieves.

In Jesus' one powerful act of submitting to John's baptism, he was legitimizing the people's response to religious corruption. This was no small gift. If you have been raised your whole life to think of one place as the focal point of God's presence, to think of one religious institution as being superior to any other on the face of the earth, it is a great risk to take a step outside of the boundaries and seek God in another place.

It is akin to the experience that I have been told about by people raised in the Catholic Church especially before Vatican II, who came over, for whatever reasons, to a protestant church. When you have grown up thinking your church is the only true church and that there is no salvation outside of that church, it is no small risk to make a move. In a sense, Jesus is saying to the hungry, thirsty crowds, "this is the right move for you. It is righteous for you to forsake corrupt religion and to seek God out here in the wilderness."

If you will recall, the Jordan River marked the boundary line for Israel between the wilderness wanderings and their entrance into the land of promise. As God had parted the waters of the Red Sea permitting Israel to escape from slavery, so too God had stopped the waters of the Jordan allowing Israel to pass over into the land of promise. John could have stayed in Jerusalem and baptized people in the Pool of Siloam or the Pool of Bethesda but he didn't. The people needed a new beginning. They needed to go back to their entryway into the promises of God and start over. Perhaps this new beginning was part of what Jesus referred to as fulfilling all righteousness.

The Gospel writers understood Jesus' life, death, and resurrection as both a new Genesis and a new Exodus, an exodus this time, not from Egyptian slavery, but an exodus from sin and death and from life-long bondage to the fear of death. Jesus for his part is simply saying repentance is the necessary starting point for any new beginning with God. We have a saying that says, "Insanity is doing the same thing over and over and expecting a different result." Repentance means try something new; go in a different direction.

Or as Jesus succinctly put it, "Come unto me all ye that labor and are heavy laden and I will give you rest."

Secondly, Jesus was pouring grace upon John's ministry. John has already acknowledged that Jesus' ministry was the greatest. John said water baptism for repentance was much less than Spirit baptism which would be done by the one who came after him. But Jesus graciously tied water baptism to Spirit baptism uniting them in the purpose of bringing new, abundant life. And it is still so to this day. Jesus did not throw John's faithful ministry to the side of the road. He picked baptism up and included it into his own, elevating it to the sacred sacrament we still practice.

Baptism has become, not simply an indication of the human desire for something more or the human effort to do better. Baptism in water and in Spirit together seals us as God's beloved and as family members in the household of faith. Righteousness is fulfilled through a sacrament which unites the earthly element of water with the heavenly element of the Holy Spirit. "All righteousness" is incarnational through and through. You might say our faith has its feet planted firmly on the ground and our hearts soaring through heavenly skies.

Thirdly, Jesus fulfilled all righteousness and perfected all grace by emptying himself, taking the form of a servant as Paul wrote in Philippians. Jesus could have kept his distance. He could have looked down, approving of all the hunger and remorse of the miserable sinners coming for baptism. He could have staked his claim among the pack of judgmental snakes hovering on the banks who were taking in the religious show. He could have been a scrupulous tongue-clucker, shaking his head and wagging his finger at human frailty and failure to become righteous on our own strength. But he didn't.

A Fellowship of Cracked Pots

To fulfill all righteousness, to show just how committed God was to our wellbeing, he came down into the baptismal waters, those waters filled with human sin and frustration and disappointment, those waters polluted by all violence and hatred and unforgiveness, with all harshness and lack of mercy and compassion, he got thoroughly drenched as he identified with the human condition. He became one with us. And rather than making himself dirty by association with us, he took the dirt upon himself to bear it away and to transform a dead-end street into the way.

Jesus fulfilled all righteousness, not only that day in the Jordan but all the way to Golgotha where he hung on a cross devised by human wickedness. On the day of his baptism a voice came from heaven, "This is my beloved Son; with him I am well pleased." God was saying not only "I like who he is, I like what he is doing," but also, "I approve of the humility and the willingness to sacrifice his life for others. In these things, he is just like me and he is doing exactly what I want him to do."

One definition of righteousness is that it means to stand in right relationship. Unrighteousness means we are out of relationship; our relationship is somehow broken, twisted, out of shape. To become righteous means to come into right relationship. It is only grace that has the power to take the unrighteous and make us righteous. Becoming righteous is beyond our power to achieve. Righteousness always comes to us as sheer gift. Jesus gift of forgiveness and grace brings us back into the proper relationship with our God, Father, Son, and Holy Spirit. And when we are in right relationship we are free to exercise our gifts in the presence of God.

So, return now to our little imaginative exercise. There you are in the pulpit. Jesus is there, sitting in the front, affirming you and encouraging you to proceed. What will you do? Or maybe you will never be asked to preach. But you do pray. So, picture yourself in your place of prayer, and suddenly Jesus is sitting beside you. What will you say? What do you want to say? What do you dare to say? Will you be dusting off the "Thees" and "Thous" of your King James English, or will you speak naturally like a person with a friend? Did you ever really expect Jesus to show up when you set out to pray? Do you ever try to share your faith with someone? What if Jesus appeared at your side in the moment of testimony, encouraging you to "go on; I can't wait to hear what you have to say about our relationship."

Jesus could show up at your desk on Sunday morning as you decide how much to put in the offering plate later or even when you decide you can't afford to worship God with an offering. Sometimes, even the widow's mite seems out of reach to us. Or Jesus could show up as the worship leader says, "Let us sing to the Lord a new song, or an old hymn." Will he be blessed by how you invest your heart in praise? Better to sing off key than to withhold yourself because you don't feel qualified to sing.

In the end, Jesus going down into the waters of baptism is just his way of beginning to share his beloved-ness with every one of us. Whether you are preaching or praying or giving or praising or serving, do all with the knowledge that you are loved by the living God, by the God and Father of our Lord Jesus Christ, to the praise of His glory.

All Wet and All Set

When you check into a bed and breakfast in Britain, they have the quaint way of welcoming you: "Sign in here and we'll get you sorted." You've arrived as a traveler coming in from the hectic day looking for peace and rest. Getting sorted means getting settled in your room. The Bible begins with the world getting sorted, things put in their proper places. "In the beginning when God created the heavens and the earth, the earth was a formless void and darkness covered the face of the deep, while a wind from God swept over the face of the waters." Genesis 1:1-2. The wind from God was the activity of the Holy Spirit. God's creation began in primal chaos and God immediately began to get things sorted out, dividing light from darkness, sea from dry land and so on.

I've had just enough bouts with sea sickness to share ancient Israel's distrust of the waters, especially when they are churned up by the wind. The only cure for a land lubber when sea sickness strikes is land. Out on the water old Israel and I feel like we're out of our element. We like things to be sorted, each thing in its proper place. My proper place is on good old terra firma. But we can't do without water. 98% of our bodies are made up of water. We can go for long periods without food, but not without water. Without water the earth is a trackless waste. Rain in the desert can provoke a sense of wonder as the arid ground sprouts overnight and long dormant seeds of life come into glorious bloom as though by miracle or magic. An oasis with nothing but a puddle looks like a little piece of heaven to a thirsty traveler trekking through the desert. And baptism to a repentant sinner should be like a cool drink of water, refreshing and renewing.

In the Exodus story, the water of the Red Sea appeared like a barrier that would stop Israel's flight to freedom. At first, the sea looked like the agent of a watery death at Pharaoh's hands. But God made a way where there was no way then used the waters of the same sea to judge Israel's oppressors and bring them to naught.

When Israel, out in the desert of their newly won freedom looked like they would perish from thirst, God brought forth water from the rock at Moses' command. Water was both problem and blessing to the ancient Hebrews. The prophet Jonah thought to use water as his escape route from obedience to God's call. God frustrated that escape in the belly of a huge water creature giving Jonah the choice between being fish food or fish vomit unto obedience. Jonah didn't like either option but ended up living the latter in grudging obedience So today we retell one of the Bible's water stories.

We remember the Baptism of the Lord. John the Baptist conducted his ministry down in the river, preaching about repentance and dunking people under water to symbolize a turning from their old ways as a preparation for new ways soon to be revealed. "I baptize you with water," he thundered, "But after me comes one who will baptize you with the Holy Spirit." All who would come were invited to a sin bath, and many did go down seeking something better than their dried up, sin soaked lives. Sadly, in the history of Christian spirituality, the Holy Spirit has made people feel more threatened than the waters of their daily chaos and the frustrations of the daily grind of lust and power games and striving to make all of our ends meet, whether financial, emotional, or spiritual ends. Maybe we don't really hate our sin as much as we say we do during our prayers of confession. So many have become so comfortable with the devil they know that they have settled for far less than God's intentions for their lives. For many it's enough just to get through another day so we can get up again tomorrow and try to make it through. Most of us have abandoned the adventure of holiness.

A Fellowship of Cracked Pots

When Jesus stepped down into the Jordan to be baptized by John, John's ministry essentially came to an end. It's not that repentance became unnecessary but that it was subsumed into a spiritual reality which is much vaster than merely turning away from sin. Jesus was baptized not as a visual admonition for people to straighten up and fly right. His baptism was his ordination service as the Lamb of God who takes away the sin of the world. He and we are baptized into something dynamically new, not just separated from the stinking old.

In his most wise and perceptive moment, John told his disciples, "He must increase and I must decrease." I wonder why John didn't just throw down his hair shirt and follow Jesus. I wonder why he kept on preaching about repentance. I wonder why he felt compelled to confront Herod about his immoral taking of his own brother's wife as his own. Was it sheer momentum that kept him thundering against sin after Jesus came as the one to take it away? Did he really have to lose his head? Did John think that the main purpose of the Church was to function as the morality police? Possibly.

Many Christians today have no deeper vision for faith that this. They see it as their job to uncover the sins that the blood of Christ was shed to cover. But what if the Christian Gospel cuts much deeper than the issues of morality and ethics? Morality and ethics are important to be sure, but is that all there is to our faith? Is it just a system of rules and regulations to get everyone to behave? I think it is much deeper and much more revolutionary than that.

In our text from Acts 19, Paul came to Ephesus and found some people who said they believed in Jesus. Lots of people say they believe in Jesus, but Paul was insightful enough to want to know a little more before he shouted "Hallelujah!" So, he asked them this crucial question: "Did you receive the Holy Spirit when you believed?" And their telltale answer was, "No, we have never even heard that there is a Holy Spirit." It turns out that they were only baptized into John's baptism of repentance. The focus was solely upon turning away from sin. But turning toward what? Paul led them deeper and they were baptized with the Holy Spirit and spoke with tongues and prophesied. It was like Acts 2 in Jerusalem all over again.

This whole phenomenon of speaking in tongues has sparked all sorts of controversy in the church, along with much suspicion, a bunch of fear, and a great deal of false teaching. Sometimes tongues are another language known among human beings, spoken by someone who never studied, let's say Portuguese or Swahili. Sometimes tongues are ecstatic speech unknown to any. The Bible records both kinds of occurrences. Paul says in I Corinthians 13, "If I speak in the tongues of men or of angels...." I wonder if most of us though, even the most open and sympathetic to this gift, haven't missed the major point.

As many of you know, I've been trying to learn Spanish in preparation for my pilgrimage across Spain. I've learned some. I know that a chair is una cilla, a bed is una cama, that the restroom is el banjo and how to ask where it is (donde esta el banjo), and that cold water is agua freia. This exercise is simply applying different words for a known reality.

But when we are reborn in Christ, set free from sin and death, and invited to participate in a new kind of life, it's hard at first to talk about it to people who still don't know Christ. From the moment, we are born again and are baptized in the Holy Spirit, we begin to receive revelation about God, who God is, what is God's character, and we begin to discern God's will. As we grow we are guessing less and less because we are hearing more and more, and what we are hearing does not make sense to the unregenerate man or woman. Spiritual language sounds foolish to them. We might as well be speaking in tongues.

It's been almost exactly a year since my dear friend Barbara in California died. If you were here last winter I told you about Jean's and my trip to San Diego the week before she died and some of what it meant to me. A couple of days ago, I called her husband Ron to see how he was doing. I must say I was pleasantly surprised to hear what he said.

Barbara was a deeply spiritual lady, very sensitive to the Holy Spirit and very insightful. While she was alive, it's as though Ron simply consulted the Lord through her. But now, since she's been gone, he has learned to commune with the Lord for himself. He spends time daily communicating with the Lord. He is receiving all sorts of wisdom and direction. In his words, "My heart has grown to ten times the size that it was before Barbara died." He is carrying on the counseling practice that Barbara started and is about to close on a million-dollar office building. He said "Barbara was such a saver. I asked the Lord why he was leading me to go into such a huge debt. His answer was "because I want you to be totally dependent upon me and totally committed to this ministry." Ron used to be extremely quiet and shy. Now he is anything but. He has such joy and excitement in Jesus he's like a man reborn, and I guess he is. It was inspiring to me.

Jesus' baptism presents to our view in a nutshell the Gospel pattern of dying and rising. All the flesh can see or imagine is the dying. The flesh has no vision for resurrection realities. The natural man or woman can understand repentance, but has a much harder time with Grace. The natural man or woman has no problem understanding guilt and shame and justice and punishment for all wrong doing. Ethics are within the reach of the unredeemed. They let their conscience be their guide, and that's fine as far as it goes, but it goes neither far enough nor deep enough.

Martin Luther said something very profound: "God's main problem is not with our sin, it's with our righteousness." You remember when the Pharisee and the Publican came to church one day. The Pharisee was down in the front, thanking God that he was not wicked like the Publican, while the Publican wouldn't even look up. Jesus said the Publican was the one who went home justified. He knew he had no righteousness of his own. Right standing with God and us is gift from start to finish. Our pride in our own virtue merely blocks the way of the Holy Spirit.

This pattern made no sense to the religious people of Jesus day and makes no sense to them in our day. For many, religion is about right behavior. It is performance based. When Jesus enacted the pattern of dying and rising that day in the Jordan, as he emerged from the waters, the Spirit was revealed to descend and a voice came from heaven saying, "This is my beloved Son. In him I am well pleased."

Repentance has an important place in our Christian walk. We should practice it as long as we live, since we seem to sin as long as we live. But your sin does not puzzle God, because Grace is the centerpiece of God's plan. Your response to the Grace of Jesus Christ is important, but of prime importance is the fact that we are found lost people, and we are found because "he has sought us and bought us with his redeeming blood" as the hymn puts it.

Let me close by reading three verses from I John 5:6-8: This is he who came by water and blood, Jesus Christ, not with the water only but with the water and the blood. And the Spirit is the witness, because the Spirit is the truth. There are three witnesses, the Spirit, the water, and the blood; and these three agree." The

Holy Spirit within us speaks to us of the saving work of Christ and applies it to our whole life. The water of Jesus' baptism preaches his solidarity with us, and declares that God is for us. Therefore, who can stand against us? It is the very picture of our dying and rising life in Christ. And the blood witnesses to the length that God will go to reclaim us as his very own beloved sons and daughters.

The Baptism of the Lord is a day worth marking, worth remembering, and worth celebrating. Just as our baptism inaugurates us into a new kind of life, so Jesus' baptism brought him full into his mission to become our Savior and Lord.

And the Winner Is

New Year's Day, Valentine's Day, St. Patrick's Day, Mother's Day, Memorial Day, Father's Day, Fourth of July, Labor Day, Halloween, Veteran's Day, Thanksgiving, shopping days left until Christmas, your birthday, perhaps your anniversary, your vacation days, the first days of Spring, Summer, Fall, and Winter, springing forward to daylight savings time and falling back to Eastern Standard time, oh and don't forget to mention family birthdays and other special occasions—these give shape and rhythm to a typical year. As Tom Rush sang in his song Circle Game: "the seasons, they go 'round and 'round; the painted ponies go up and down; we're captive on the carousel of time. We can't return we can only look, behind from where we came, and go round and round in the circle game." And oh, don't the circles speed up, going faster and faster as our lives pile up their years? We use all kinds of markers to give shape, meaning, and a sense of order to the chaos of our day to day lives.

As a pastor, I'm like a broken record at this point (if you are too young to know what a broken record is, ask your grandpa). I tell you every year that Christ the King Sunday is one of my favorite markers in the Christian year. We have once again come full circle, beginning late last year with Advent, the season of nurturing our hope and expectations of the coming Christ, at his birth and at his final appearing. We celebrated his birth, moved into Epiphany to commemorate his being revealed to the wider world outside of Israel. Wise men, gentile astrologers, came from the east bearing gifts and offering worship. We spent the long penitent season of Lent, arriving at Holy Week both chastened and needing comfort. We have considered the agony of the Cross and the ecstasy of Easter. We've journeyed along through the great fifty days, marking the Ascension of Christ on day forty and the outpouring of the Holy Spirit on Pentecost, fifty days after Easter.

Then came the longest stretch of all through ordinary time, and if we are growing up at all in Christ, we are increasingly cognizant that it is precisely in ordinary time when many extraordinary things are given. As we mature in Christ, we begin to discover that all of our life is potentially sacred, and we begin to notice as well how much of ordinary life has been desecrated. The busyness of our desecrated calendars can, if we are not alert, empty our lives of their intended meaning which comes to us as a gift from God.

God's intention for each one of us is to live an abundant life, but too many of us have become settlers, people who settle for less, who have come to accept spiritual scarcity as an acceptable norm, and who have simply allowed God and the things of God to be pushed to the margins of our lives. What is appointed by God to be sacred about us becomes de-sacreded—desecrated.

To establish a day where we acknowledge and proclaim, "Christ the King," can function as a loud, "Hold everything! All you who say you are Christians listen up! To say Jesus Christ is Lord must never become empty words. That confession demands involvement, commitment to a kind of life called discipleship. It compels participation in God's work through all the seasons of our lives."

Whoever or whatever you name as Lord in your life is never content with leftovers. If your lord is money, you will give most of your time and energy toward making it, more and more and more of it. If your lord is entertainment, you will be working furiously so you can afford to buy it. Entertainment is usually pretty expensive. If you are your own lord, you'll spend your energy, intelligence, imagination, and love propping up your own ego in some way or another. Sooner or later, in the mercy of God, all of our service to lords spelled with a small "l" will be revealed as service in the direction of a dead end. It is service to the Lord Jesus Christ that leads, not to death, but to life.

I have a confession to make. Many of you know that as I preach sermons through the church year, I follow the lectionary, which is a table of prescribed readings for each week. It is designed as a guide to help preachers like me grapple with the whole counsel of God in preaching and not just our pet texts. There are usually several options from both Old and New Testaments and often a Psalm as well. So, when I got to this week's selections, there was a choice between the Colossians 1 passage and one from the Gospel of Luke. Listen to part of the Luke passage:

When they came to the place that is called The Skull, they crucified Jesus there with the criminals, one on his right and one on his left. Then Jesus said, "Father, forgive them; for they know not what they are doing." And they cast lots to divide his clothing. And the people stood by, watching; but the leaders scoffed at him, saying, "He saved others; let him save himself if he is the Messiah of God, his chosen one!" The soldiers also mocked him, coming up and offering him sour wine, and saying, "If you are the King of the Jews, save yourself!" There was also an inscription over him, "This is the King of the Jews." Luke 23:33-38.

Now here's my confession: I was thinking how the Colossians text would be a lot more positive for reading on this open-heart Sunday. Many of you are here because someone reached out and invited you to come. In fine Presbyterian fashion, we even have a continental breakfast prepared for after worship. We want you to have a good morning. We want you to experience our joy and good will. We want all of us to experience a fine moment in the life of our congregation. We all want to see a glimpse at least of the wonderful love of God that is extended to each one of us. And on the surface, these passion narratives can seem a little depressing.

But then I was reminded that we don't look at things on the surface. By the guiding of the Holy Spirit, we have developed the habit of looking at things more deeply, below the surface. The magnificent affirmations of the text from Colossians are lofty, breath-taking even. Jesus is the image of the invisible God. All things in heaven and on earth were created by him and for him. In him all things hold together. He is the firstborn from the dead. He has first place in everything, in creation, in life, in victory over death, in making peace between God and all creatures. All the fullness of God is pleased to dwell in him. And he has delivered us from death to life. Jesus Christ is King! Hallelujah. That's a declaration we can wrap our arms willingly around with big smiles on our faces. A good time will be had by all.

But hold on. There's that bit about the coronation of God's Christ. All this glory rests upon an event gory and grisly. It takes place, not in an opulent palace hall but upon Golgotha, the place of a skull. His enthronement was not announced by the sounding of royal trumpets but by the scoffing of both secular soldiers and religious people who claimed to know God very well. He was not seated on an ornate chair covered with gold and studded with precious jewels. His throne was roughhewn wooden beams to which he was fastened with the harsh iron spikes of Roman domination and cruelty. Their king ruled by might and the threat of violence. This king, the King of the Jews, Christ our king, ruled through meekness, kindness, humility, through love that was willing to suffer the ultimate torment and the epitome of public scorn and mocking derision.

I ask you, what kind of way is this to wrap up the church year? And I ask you another question: can you think of a better, more honest way to do so? For it is in the willing suffering of Jesus the Christ that we see most profoundly the depth of God's love for us. Even on the cross prepared by his own creatures upon which to hang their creator, we hear him praying for our forgiveness, taking our ignorance into account and submitting it to his own powerful and longsuffering kindness.

And logically, we may even see that without death, there is no resurrection, and resurrection is really the heart of the matter. If there is no resurrection wrote Paul, our faith is futile and we are still in our sins. We are still at the mercy of all the little "I" lords we have appointed to lead us around, so we can eat, drink, and be merry, with no greater future than our certain death tomorrow.

So, let me say it again, the lofty affirmations of Christ the King we read in Colossians, stand upon the events of Jesus' passion. In a totally unexpected and unforeseen way, the gruesome events of Good Friday formed the gateway to the glories unleashed on Easter Day, glories that have continued on down through the ages and have overtaken people like you and me in the here and now.

My dear friends, we have a wonderful faith dearly bought. Our very God and our creator has become our redeemer and our King. Our King Jesus is nothing but good, wills nothing but good for us, is infinitely kind, and breathtakingly merciful.

With that message, our hearts are now prepared to begin all over again. Advent begins next Sunday. The season of renewal is upon us. It is another season to see our hopes reborn, our faith deepened, and our love for God and for one another revitalized. If you came today as a sort of cameo appearance, may I invite you to think about it a little more? Those of us who come here on a regular basis would be so much richer if you would continue on with us on the journey of faith. Your gifts, your life, you are particularly unique. We miss you when you are absent. We are blessed when you are present. Would you pray about taking your place in the church family in a new way? Whatever you decide, know that you are not forgotten. Know that you are in our prayers. And never forget that God is relentlessly for you and ceaselessly longs for your heart to be open and receptive to the love that God offers through Christ the King.

Big Things from Small Beginnings

News flash from the suburbs: my neighbors have a back lawn. You say, "What kind of headline is that? Doesn't everyone in Cherry Hill have a lawn?" To which I reply, "Almost everyone but me. I have what you might call a lot." I remember when the previous owners of my neighbor's house got their lawn. Crews came in. The ground was scraped, aerated, and covered with sod. Watering became mandatory. Chem-Lawn crews came periodically and sprayed chemicals all over the place. It must have cost thousands of dollars.

Call me Mr. Natural. As I sat on my deck sipping a cold drink and beholding this beehive of transformation and labor and expenditure I had a smug sense of true moral superiority. My lot is low cost, low maintenance, and completely organic! Oh, I did make a halfhearted attempt a few times to keep up with the neighbors. I bought some super-duper guaranteed to grow anywhere grass seed and threw it around my lot. But to no avail. I blamed the failure on the dogs we had at the time.

The recently deceased king of the blues, B. B. King had a lyric, "If it wasn't for bad luck people, I wouldn't have no luck at all." I've stolen it and adjusted it to say, "If it wasn't for crabgrass people, I wouldn't have no grass at all." Well, that's enough of that foolish talk, even if Cyndy Lauper almost sang, "Preachers just want to have fun." Let's get serious now.

I want to talk to you about something Jesus was always talking about, the Kingdom of God. He talked about the Kingdom of God more than anything else. He told people about it often in little time bomb stories called parables. These little stories with their pedestrian similes and metaphors seem almost bland and innocuous. They are simple, everyday stories with no big words. All the farmers in the listening crowds found them easy to understand. It was the religious sophisticates that had the most trouble with them.

Eugene Peterson in his volume of spiritual theology entitled, Tell It Slant, parses the word parable. He says it is a combination of two Greek words, *para*, which means alongside, and *bole*, which means thrown. A parable then is something that is thrown alongside us. And by its simple nature it is puzzling. When we come across it, we are likely to say, "What's that doing here. How did it get here? And what's the point? What in the world is Jesus talking about?" Those are actually the questions that Jesus wants his hearers to ask. As I said, parables are like little time bombs. They take a while to go off in our minds and hearts. Then, when you least expect it, "Boom;" they go off.

A minute ago, I just lobbed a few of these little stories in your direction. Let's look for a moment at just one of them. In Mark 4:26-29 we have a parable in three short verses which tells us what the Kingdom of God is like. Jesus says in 74 words what scholars have written about in huge tomes of theological reflection and study. "What's the Kingdom of God like Jesus?" "It's like Bill Gaskill throwing seeds around on his lot. He then goes to sleep; he rises the next day, sleeps the next night, gets up again. This goes on day after day. After he tosses the seed on the ground, it's out of his hands so to speak. It's the same with Kingdom of God seed. But unlike Bill's seed, Kingdom of God seed actually begins to sprout and grow."

Let's not get ahead of ourselves here. Short parables invite us to slow down. If Jesus says only a few words to illustrate his favorite subject, I get suspicious that there is a lot more to them than at first meets the eye. And if I may say so in all humility, I'm right about it this time. Let's dig a little deeper. Think about seed planting. Usually, seeds are not very big. In the next parable about God's kingdom in Mark, Jesus uses as his example the mustard seed, the smallest of all seeds in his day. Somehow seeds must be sown. And somehow, they need to get down under some soil if they are going to do well. The soil needs some preparation, some roughing up, some way to create a hole, or a furrow, or even a small crevice for the seed to fall into.

The seed goes down into the dark. There tiny microbes attack the seed's protective hull, trying to crack it open, break down its defenses, so that the life inside is free to come out. Isn't it ironic how the defenses we construct which seem so useful at the time we build them to defend us from hurt or disappointment of some kind have to be dismantled by the Holy Spirit so that our true self can emerge into the light of day? Ego defenses tend to become prison walls if we don't allow them to be torn down. Sooner or later, they have to go.

I know you know that the Kingdom of God is not the name of a geographical place. It is a title signifying God's sovereignty. The kingdom is all about spiritual authority. And the vehicle for that authority is the Gospel. Jesus in his person brings that authority to earth, special delivery. The seed that is planted in the soil of your life and mine is Gospel seed. Jesus is that seed in person. The good news, which is what "gospel" means, is not a tack on to the Kingdom of God. The Kingdom of God, the sovereign will of God, the divine authority that enters our life's soil, the holiness of God's rule, is the central and vibrant, life giving reality that is sown into your heart and mine. It is implanted there by faith in Jesus Christ. And then the transformation that every one of us requires to be fit for the Kingdom of God takes on a life of its own. When we receive the Grace of God, when our lives have Gospel seed sown into them, things begin to happen, things of which we are not in charge.

One of the earliest lessons I learned on the Camino was that this ancient path would not submit to my will. It was vast, and unchangeable. I had to discover and accept what millions of pilgrims have found out before me. I had to submit to it. If the road went up, I had to climb. If the way was rough, I had to slow down, or pay the price in pain. If the weather was hot, I took off some clothing. If it poured rain, out came the rain gear. I had to find my own pace, my own self if you will, and stay within it. One of the first lessons of Kingdom of God living is always humility. God resists the proud but gives grace to the humble. So, the Bible says. If you are going to walk with Jesus, this is pretty much step one.

When Gospel seed enters our sin-darkened lives, the attack upon the seed commences. Like Jacob wrestling with the angel of the Lord, our flesh resists another lord tooth and nail. Spiritual life is always contested by the unholy trinity of the world, the flesh, and the devil. And in God's sovereign majesty, God even causes God's enemies to serve the Gospel. All spiritual resistance notwithstanding, there in the dark where sin's microbes attack our new life, the hulls of our sin nature begin to crack and give way to the plan and purpose of the Kingdom of God being applied by the ministry of the Holy Spirit. The next thing you know, a blade, green and full of potential peeks up into the light of day. Jesus says that we don't know exactly how this happens, but we can see evidence that seed and soil are beginning to act together to bring forth life and hopefully grow all the way to fruit bearing and an eventual harvest.

As I was walking along in Galicia one morning, I saw a farmer walking through a field of very young corn plants. All the rows seemed complete with tender shoots just where you would expect them to be. I waved and called in my version of Spanish, "Su compo es muy bueno!" Your field is beautiful and full of promise is what I meant. He returned a friendly enough shrug. Later I realized that his crop was a long way from fruit bearing. Spain had experienced severe drought in the previous year, and this year was starting off very dry. Every farmer knows his crop is dependent upon forces way beyond his control. Along with the farmer's skill, good weather, adequate rain, and resistance to pests and plant diseases all are required.

So, it is with our growth in the Kingdom. Many things we don't control come into play. We learn sooner or later that we must trust the creator of life and the Lord of the harvest to bring us from blade, to ear, to fullness in fruit bearing, to our destination of bearing ripe fruit which then becomes a bountiful harvest for God in this world. There is a rhythm and pace to spiritual life. There is as much timing involved as there is in a beautiful piece of music.

People then were not so different from people now. Most of them and most of us would prefer instant deliverance, instant holiness, and instant sanctification. They wanted their Messiah then to come and foment a cataclysmic change in world government. They wanted fast food at a drive through kingdom window. Jesus is telling them in this little story that kingdom work and development is rarely like that. It is more like what every farmer knows about every crop he ever planted.

The kingdom of God is dependent upon God. This is the true meaning of the virgin birth. It is not so much a biological miracle, though it is that, but a theological statement by God. God is informing the world that it cannot save itself. The world, in order to be saved from sin and death needs to be invaded from outside itself. So, God, in the form of the smallest of invisible seeds enters the world through the virgin's womb, and from there, look what has happened. The seed of grace has grown into a very large plant, into a visible representation of the Kingdom of God.

The Kingdom of God begins down out of sight, whether in a stable in Bethlehem or in a heart like yours and mine. The Kingdom of God, King Jesus, does first things first. The Kingdom of God, King Jesus, will deal with the darkness of our own sin nature by assuming it in himself and taking it all the way to the Cross. There it is nailed up in judgment and put to death, in and by Jesus.

The Kingdom of God will insist on touching not only your guilt but your shame. It takes real courage for us to submit to this ministry of the King. Richard Rohr speaks of how each of us must learn to face our own shadow, the dark underbelly of our public mask. Under the glittering image of our own self-produced personality there lies hidden from public view a vast array of flaws. Rohr says if we don't confront our own darkness, we will continually be pointing to the darkness in others. We know the darkness is there. If we refuse to face what's in us, we go looking for it, and of course it is easy to find in a world full of sinners, every one of whom needs redeemed.

The only people who fail to see grace as amazing are the people who still have the illusion that they don't need it. These are the ones who see themselves as a cut above the rest of fallen humanity. These are the people who try to find their place among people by figuring out whom they consider to be worse than themselves and who they fear are better than themselves.

Kingdom citizens are no longer shame based, guilt ridden people. We no longer need to compare our righteousness to that of another because we have discovered that we have no other righteousness than that given to us by our association with the King, Jesus, who is our Savior, the Lord of Lords and the King of kings. Kingdom citizens are people who have been set free and forgiven. Kingdom citizens know without a doubt that the will of their sovereign is that they bear much fruit and visibly manifest the fact that they have become disciples of Jesus. We are people who are learning how to function as fully redeemed human beings.

Jesus is trying in these few words to alert people like you and me that the Kingdom of God and the life it conveys may not at first look like much. It often, perhaps most often, begins as humbly as a small seed. But the kingdom has an inner vitality which is full of promise and under the power of God will lead to a fruitful harvest of righteousness. Friends, you and I have been granted citizenship in the Kingdom of God. Sleep at night, and then rise each new day you are given to see how the plants are growing. You may begin to see miracles all around you.

Coffee and the Paper Are Not Enough

I never, ever watch award shows, those self-congratulatory, narcissistic, ego parades staged by the *prima donnas* of our cultural elites, so called. I have seen the reports though. The stars and starlets roll up in a limousine and place their pretty little feet delicately on the red carpet. They parade up the aisle amidst adoring fans, ravenous photographers, and jealous critics hungry to notice some fatal flaw in makeup or fashion so that they can pick them apart later with a withering critique designed to tumble these idols from atop their perches on top of Mount Olympus and see them roll down among the rest of us mortals. That dress was hideous. She showed too much skin. What is he still doing with her? Is the rumor true that they are breaking up, that he is cheating, that she is about to dump him? He's gotten wrinkles. She's put on a few pounds. On and on it goes.

I guess Palm Sunday seemed more like a night at the Oscars, first century style, than what it actually was. Instead of red carpet, substitute palm fronds, human cloaks, and leafy branches, laid down to carpet the path of the Messiah, the Son of David come at last to deliver the beleaguered Jews from the hated Roman occupiers. "Hosanna!" they shouted. "Blessed is he who comes in the name of the Lord!" He was that crowd's version of American idol. In their enthusiasm, they failed to notice that Jesus' robe was seamless but certainly not a designer item. And it seemed incidental that Jesus was seated on a borrowed donkey's colt; he didn't even own it!

The people that day made the mistake many have made in every age since Jesus came. Somehow, they failed to notice that Jesus emptied himself on that day, just like he had been doing every day since his nativity. The whole experience of becoming human was a sacrifice of love from start to finish. Incarnation was colossally expensive beyond our ability to calculate, but don't think of it as some kind of afterthought that came as a surprise to Jesus. In fact, the Bible tells us that the divine self-emptying has been going on since before the foundation of the world. Sacrificial love is not a tack on to the character of our Almighty and most holy God. Self-emptying love is the hallmark of the nature and character of God. When we say God is love, we might recall Paul's words in I Corinthians 13: "Love does not insist on its own way." There is no instance where that love becomes domineeringly self-centered. Father, Son, and Holy Spirit are by nature sacrificial lovers. Our awesome God knows how to accomplish God's will and purpose and plan through becoming a servant. Astounding!

The Palm Sunday parade into Jerusalem is often referred to as the Triumphal entry of Jesus into the Holy City. But let's be clear here. This event is triumphal in the same sense that Good Friday is good. On the first Good Friday, those who loved and followed Jesus would never have called it good. It was the worst day and the first day of the rest of their lives which promised to be nothing but empty and defeated. Those who had bet their lives upon Jesus felt as though they'd lost it all, and for what? They had no framework with which to connect the gruesome spectacle of Christ crucified with goodness or victory, not until Easter morning when the resurrection changed everything decisively once and for all. When God forged an indissoluble link between death and resurrection, horrible Friday was transformed to Good Friday. We proclaim it still.

In himself, Jesus knew that this parade was no victory lap, not yet. How hollow the shouts of acclamation would have sounded had he not known the plan. He knew he was headed for the cross in just a few short days. He knew that once the people became disappointed in him and disillusioned by him, they would feel tricked and deceived and instead of "Hosanna" they would raise the shrill cry, "Crucify!" But the Bible tells us that Jesus, because of the glory set before him, because he could see the triumph even in face of his imminent suffering, not in the ability to avoid the cross which he most certainly had the power to muster on his own behalf, he had the firmness of resolve he needed to endure the cross in order to achieve his purpose of dying for the sins of the whole world. That includes your sin and my sin. Jesus emptied himself. In his own earthly body, a body just like ours, Jesus suffered and died, the innocent for the guilty, the sinless for the sin filled. And oh what fullness has issued from that act of emptying!

Because Jesus emptied himself and took on human form, because he was obedient to the plan and purpose of God even when that plan led him all the way to an agonizing death, and because this precious being who did no wrong ever and healed the broken and fed the hungry and had compassion on many, and because he emptied himself of every single privilege of divinity, the emptiness of sin and death was definitively exposed as an imposter and an unwelcome intruder in the Kingdom of God and of God's good creation.

Because Jesus emptied himself, when the women ran to the garden tomb on the first Easter morn, the tomb was empty. Jesus emptied himself in death and the result was that death was emptied of its power. Because Jesus emptied himself and died, the creation received the ability to be filled up with all the fullness of God. We might properly say that Jesus real triumphal entry was when they laid him in the tomb. He descended into hell; the third day he rose again from the dead.

Theologians have told us that the first thing Jesus did after his death was to do what they describe as harrowing hell. He went to the darkest realm to begin to claim the spoils of his victory. In the

Apostle's Creed we say, "He descended into hell." Peter tells us that after his death on the cross Jesus went and preached the Gospel to the spirits who were in prison. Jesus went down even into the pit to set the captives free. Jesus goes to the uttermost depths of darkness to shine the divine light of God's redemptive purpose. If this is what Jesus does when he is empty, when he has been crucified, dead, and buried, can you even begin to imagine what he will be like when we meet him full once more of all his divine glory. Read the book of Revelation if you want a sneak preview.

"But," you say, "what does all this high-sounding rhetoric have to do with me? These tales you tell, even if they are true, happened a long time ago in a land far away. How can this be relevant to my daily life, going to work, being a good husband, a good wife, a good parent, a good child, paying the taxes, painting the house and cutting the lawn?"

Before I attempt an answer, let me ask you a question, and a very important question at that. Here it is; are you ready? How big of a life do you really want? And here are a few others to go along with it: Are you content to live a life that is small, banal, trivial, a life that is frittered away seeking the sops and trinkets that the world tosses your way to pacify you spiritually and keep you docilely managing your own despair? You say, "Whoa Pastor Bill, that doesn't describe me. I'm a mensch. I'm a rugged individual. I'm a character. I'm my own man, my own woman. I do what I want and I'm satisfied, thank you very much." God bless you, I'm not.

In the recent issue of The Christian Century, William Brosend reports on an interview he had with the renowned preacher Fred Craddock. Mr. Craddock has gone on to the Lord just since that article was written. In the interview, Fred Craddock told of the following incident: "I was walking down a sidewalk in Decatur,

A Fellowship of Cracked Pots

Georgia, on the way to the church where I was to preach when I met an acquaintance sitting at an outdoor coffee shop. We chatted and she asked me to join her, but I said that I needed to get to church. I invited her to join me, but she held up her Sunday paper and said, 'This is my Bible,' and then her coffee cup, 'This is my communion.'" Craddock then said, "I think the days of that nonsense are ending. I believe that our traditions are going to return with strength, both to the Eucharist and to carefully crafted sermons that will demand to be published and reread after they are heard." Brosend said then, "He knows that coffee and the Sunday Times are not sufficient." So, I ask you again, "Are you satisfied?

Brosend then quoted Craddock further: "the question is not whether the church is dying, but whether it is giving its life for the world. If the Son of Man came not to be served but to serve others, might that not be a proper starting place for the proclamation of the Son of Man?"

If you want a bigger, more vibrant, more significant life, you are going to have to get it the way Jesus got it. You are going to have to empty yourself. If you don't empty yourself, you will never discover the joys of serving either God or human beings. You will deprive yourself of the fruitfulness that comes from serving Jesus Christ. You will become incarcerated in stinking pride, stinking thinking, stinking priorities, in stinking selfishness that tries to find meaning in paltry pursuits that have no lasting, eternal value. You will labor in vain and all will be buried with you when you leave this earth.

Maybe you've already discovered what I have discovered. I've read thousands of papers in my life. I've probably drunk a hundred thousand cups of coffee. They filled my head with information, much of it useless, and my body with little jolts of energy and moments of enjoyment. None of it has lasted.

But following Christ is so much deeper, so much more satisfying than anything the world has to offer. I've discovered that the more I empty myself, the fuller I become. I hear this process spoken of today, not in the words, "Empty yourself." What is now said is, "Get over yourself."

One of the lessons of Palm Sunday is that the path to triumph in God passes through the Cross. If you want to be exalted, you must first be humbled. Humility does not come naturally to us. There is always pride which must be crucified on the way to becoming humble. You and I must be taught how to forsake our inherent self-love which is manifested in selfishness in order to become established as deeply loved, beloved children of the Living God. It is as the Beloved of God that we tap into the joys of the spiritual life, of worship, and of generosity, and of service.

On Sunday, your only day to sleep in, rise late, and drink a leisurely cup of coffee, read the paper and do the crossword puzzle, on the days when life's simple pleasures seem to be enough, maybe then is when we need to be most careful. Don't let the seductive powers of the things of this world, not bad in and of themselves, be the reason you forsake the worship of God. When you sum it up by saying, "I missed church today," it's most likely that you will have missed a whole lot more. Coffee and the paper are not enough.

Coming, Going, Coming Again

This past Thursday was the day in the liturgical year known as the Feast of the Ascension. I'll bet most of you didn't know that and also that most of us have no clue as to why we should care. We can make the case for coming to worship on Maundy Thursday, falling in the midst of Holy Week as it does. But what Presbyterian makes much of The Ascension? Rather than spend a bunch of time and resources whining and begging you all to come to a special service last Thursday, I thought it would be easier to commandeer this seventh Sunday of Easter to think together about it.

The only New Testament writer who tells the story is Luke, and he thinks so much of it that he tells the story twice, once at the end of his gospel, and again in the beginning of his second account of the work of Christ in the Acts. Luke must have thought this was very important. In Acts Luke is writing to Theophilus, whose name means "lover of God" his further account of all that Jesus began to do and teach. The Acts is his account of the ongoing work of Jesus by the Holy Spirit through the newborn church and her apostles. The Gospel of Luke and Acts are like a two-volume set of what Luke wants to say is crucial to "God lovers" everywhere.

In the Bible, first things and last things tend to carry extra weight. One of the last things Luke talks about in his gospel is the account of Jesus disappearing from the disciples' sight for the last time, forty days after Easter. And one of the first things he recounts again in Acts is the same event. Jesus is taken up from their sight with the promise that he would come and be among them in a new way, "not many days from now." "Wait," Jesus said, "until you are clothed with power from on high." On the fiftieth day after Easter, the Day of Pentecost, the Holy Spirit would be poured out on all flesh.

Try to imagine the context of this event, of the Ascension, with me for a moment. Think with me about the plot line of the Gospel story. We could and probably should begin in Genesis and work our way forward but there isn't time today. Let's just take it back to Christmas.

Israel was groaning under the domination of yet another foreign conqueror, Rome. Rome wasn't the first foreign occupier of Israel but was the oppressor de jure. And the people were longing for the Messiah to come and set them free. We Christians, including the very first disciples of Jesus, believe that as unlikely and unexpected as was Jesus' nativity in a stable in a small crowded village, God became human in the very same way you and I became human, born of woman, though conceived by God. Jesus was God's idea not Mary's and not Joseph's: God's. But then don't we believe that along with the procreative urges of our mothers and fathers, each of us before conception were also God's idea. None of us are here by accident. Our conception and birth were wrought in God.

But we also believe that Jesus' humanity was unique among us in that it was totally untainted by sin. In the whole wide world, the humanity of us all has been diminished by sin. The Bible says, "All have sinned and fallen short of the glory of God." We all contend with life in a depleted condition. That's why we all sooner or later experience life as a difficult struggle against many things like sin and sickness and death, and like foolishness and poor choices and broken promises. The list is long.

Jesus in his full, undiminished humanity was among us as victor. But his victory was cloaked in the humility of a slave who washed the feet of his students. In his march through the world infested with unrighteousness and injustice and human arrogance and pride, he looked more like a victim than a victor. In hindsight, we know that the only reason even death seemed to defeat him for three days is that he willingly submitted to it in order to demonstrate his total mastery over it. But the disciples didn't know that ahead of time, even though he tried to tell them.

Easter changed their mourning into dancing. And for forty glorious days, Jesus came and went among them. His appearances must have been always surprising. And they were always filled with divine purpose as Jesus sought to prepare them for the work that lay ahead of them. They must have figured that this was the way things were going to go on and on, maybe for the rest of their lives; they could expect and anticipate Jesus showing up from time to time to set them straight, to give them counsel, wisdom, direction, and healing grace when they needed it. They must have been grinning from ear to spiritual ear like Cheshire cats in the Kingdom of God.

Then came the fateful day, the Day of Ascension. It would be the last time they would experience his bodily presence among them until the great day when all things become new. Two thousand years since then have passed and we are still waiting for the promise to be fulfilled that the kingdoms of this world will become the kingdom of our God and of His Christ.

When Jesus was born, John tells us "the Word became flesh and dwelt among us full of grace and truth." Jesus brought divinity from God and planted it firmly in the heart of humanity. In the ascension, Jesus took humanity and planted it smack dab in the throne room of divinity. Jesus is at once totally like us except for sin and totally unlike us because he is thoroughly divine. He is the God/man. And he has appointed it to faith in him that believing we may have life in his name. In other words, the true path to us becoming fully human in accordance with God's plan has been opened to us. Jesus lives in the presence of Father and Holy Spirit as resurrected humanity.

The ascension essentially marks the season where Jesus for the time being at least is out of sight, but not out of mind, not out of heart. He said, "I will never leave you nor forsake you. Lo, I am with you always to the close of the age."

Those ten days between Ascension and Pentecost must have seemed like an eternity. Waiting on God usually does. A thousand years might seem like a day to God, the God who is the creator and sovereign Lord of time itself, but to us mere humans, some days seem like a thousand years.

I'm reminded of how long the Saturday between Good Friday and Easter must have seemed to the grieving, disconsolate disciples, cowering behind locked doors for fear and crushed by the seeming abject defeat of the Cross. What a long, dark, endless day. And can you imagine how long the ten days between Ascension and Pentecost must have seemed. They were told to wait. So, they got together and worshipped and prayed. Jesus said they would be endued with power from on high not many days from the moment he promised it. Wait.

Could we be honest with one another for just a moment? How many of us like to wait on God or anything else for that matter? We are an instant culture. We like fast food, fast cars, fast service, fast results, fast computers, fast everything. And we live fast-lane lives just trying to keep up. We've gone from restless to frantic at the speed of darkness. To most of us who make appointments for God, God always seems to show up late. We think, "Look God you told me to pray and I have. Where is the answer? You told me to call upon you in the time of trouble and I did. Why then is life still so hard? I've waited long enough." As author Gail Ramshaw wrote in her recent article in The Christian Century about the ascension, "The mobs that worshipped on Easter Day have gone back home, and we do not yet see the universe made new."

Probably they got tired of waiting. Or perhaps they had no real expectation of a change of life in light of the resurrection to begin with.

The period between the Ascension and Pentecost is like a waiting room, as is the period between Pentecost and the full and final appearance of the risen Christ to make all things new. The question is, "What are we to do while we wait? Is waiting upon the Lord strictly passive, a season of twiddling our thumbs until the great day of the Lord comes or we go to heaven? Or is this the training season where we learn how to do justice and to love mercy and to walk humbly with our God as the prophet Micah described God's requirement of us so long ago?

To observe the ascension and to preach its meaning is to preach good news. Christ Jesus has been seated on the throne of all creation. As his will is being done in heaven, his reign is being and will finally be fully established upon the earth where we live and love one another. It's a reality worth waiting for, as we are filled with power from on high and as we give ourselves wholeheartedly to a keen expectation that what God has promised, God will deliver. Amen.

Creative Crying

For everything there is a season, and a time for every purpose under heaven…a time to laugh and a time to cry. So, wrote the preacher in Ecclesiastes. What time would you say it is now? It seems to me that by the mercy of God we are still in the in-between time. We still are able to laugh sometimes and cry at others. For some people, like Jeremiah or a Syrian refugee or a Christian about to be beheaded by a hostile extremist, the time for laughter has come and gone from their lives. But even here in the in-between times, there is a time to cry.

I don't know about you, but I find people who only relate to me on a joking level frustrating. I tend to want more from my relationships, even casual ones, than a perpetual "yuk" fest. I want to get down to things that matter, that have the potential to make me cry or at least illicit some kind of genuine concern. After a while I get the sneaking suspicion that the jokester is hiding from me, shunning real transparency and an open willingness to trust me with vulnerability. I want to say at last, "Let's get real for a moment here."

Crying tends to be a tricky thing in our macho culture, especially for men. In my formative years, I might be permitted to cry a little, especially if I was hurt in some way. But if the crying was viewed by an attending adult as superfluous, the threatening question would come: "Do you want me to give you something to cry about?" Every kid discerns the thinly veiled threat of some sort of violence to their posterior regions, or in many cases, something much worse. Most adults have a low tolerance for nuisance crying. Whining is even worse.

I clearly remember hearing a sermon by a famous TV preacher, who could cry at just the right place in every sermon when it served his homiletical purpose, saying one day that God hates whiners. Shortly thereafter, he was busted for cruising for and consorting with prostitutes. He was ruined and later both whined and cried on national TV. I don't believe God hated him then nor does he hate him now. But God did certainly allow him to come to the time for crying. Sometimes in life things come to such a pass that crying is the only appropriate response.

Jeremiah preached and prophesied for forty long years to a people who refused to listen to him or to the God who inspired him. When Jeremiah was called to the ministry God told him in advance that this would be the situation. Some call Jeremiah the weeping prophet. What sometimes is missed is that behind the very human tears and heartbreak of God's prophet there are the tears of a brokenhearted God. The horrors of conquest by ruthless foreign invaders and exile to a foreign land that finally engulfed Israel were not what their loving God desired. But they in their waywardness were determined to go their own way and do their own thing. Finally, it was as though God said, "Okay, have it your way."

I hope we are all at this point smart enough to know that our way over against God's way is the recipe for suffering and disaster. It is the gateway for the time to cry. They acted as though God was irrelevant and that they could get away with any religious thing they wanted. We might say they wanted something to cry about and they got it.

Now here is the pivot point and I don't want you to miss it. There is crying that is nothing but empty despair. There is a crying to be done when all hope is gone. There is a kind of crying in the abyss where a relationship that was once loving has been broken beyond repair. Some diseases are terminal. Some divorces are inevitable.

Some cruelties have no rhyme or reason; they simply crush their victims and leave them in the ditch beside the Jericho Road with no Good Samaritan in sight. As Bob Dylan's song described it some years ago, there are "tears of rage, tears of grief.... Come to me now you know we're so alone, and life is brief."

As bad as conditions were in and for Israel, this was not how Jeremiah cried. Jeremiah had learned the art of creative crying. Creative crying comes forth out of a place deeper than despair. Creative crying changes the dynamic of grief by inviting God to be a part of any situation. Creative crying is not about rage but rather about trust. Creative crying is undergirded by the conviction that what matters to us matters to God. Something creative emerges from the dynamic interplay between a human heart and the heart of God.

Jeremiah, through long and arduous training in being rejected and despised by people whom he loved, God's people and his very own people, had learned to cling to God. Clinging to God he was clinging to life. God was all he really had and God was all he really needed. In the darkest days of his life he had learned to hold on to hope.

When idols were substituted for the Living God in Israel, idols that couldn't see, hear, speak or answer any prayers, people were left to their own devices when things went south. When life had boiled over to the extreme conditions into which living godlessly always lead to sooner or later, the untrained who didn't know how to cry in God's presence would simply cave in to bitterness and resentment, to hopelessness and despair. By contrast, Jeremiah had learned to hold on to love.

Soren Kierkegaard wrote that when people refuse to live by the truth, they prepare secret hiding places for themselves and a Judas

A Fellowship of Cracked Pots

kiss for the consequences. Jeremiah played no such games with God. Jeremiah dared to keep it real even with, no especially with, God. The level of trust in his relationship was so deep that he could dare to be honest with God. He was confident enough to bring his raw emotions and deepest questionings to God.

Jeremiah said, "My joy is gone, grief is upon me, and my heart is sick." If the joy of the Lord is our strength as the Bible says, he was a man worn out. His ministry had exhausted him. He had no more strength to keep on confronting the consequences of Israel's waywardness and idolatry. All he could do was cry. "The harvest has passed" he cried, "the summer has ended, and we are not saved." It is as though you are gone entirely Lord. Israel has no king in her; divine authority is neither sought nor valued nor adhered to in any way that can be seen. Is there no balm in Gilead, no physician to bring healing?

Jeremiah cried and cried. He felt the hurt for his poor people. I have to believe that for every ounce of hurt Jeremiah felt, God carried tons of sorrow. The people were not just spurning Jeremiah; they were spurning the God who appointed and sent him. They were refusing to heed words divinely inspired. They had hardened their hearts against warnings born of love and compassion. They hid from the truth while developing religion that was itself a betrayal of the relationship to which true religion was to give shape. They had a Judas kiss ready for the consequences of their own apostasy. They were well versed in the precepts and practice of phony religion.

Jeremiah never did see the victory for which his soul must surely have pined. No preacher wants to die seeing no fruit whatsoever for their labors. Jeremiah did receive what was promised, but what was promised was that his sermons would meet with rejection throughout his whole ministry. Destruction did come. Exile of

Israel did happen. Have a nice day Jeremiah; have a nice life. How astounding it is that in spite of all that apparent failure, he was not a failure.

Jeremiah's success came through creative crying. He learned the secret of relating to God through sorrow. Lamentation was his specialty. And what he learned is open to every one of us who suffers. If you want to find God when it hurts, go where it hurts the most and begin to lament before God. Let your tears flow. There you will find God with you and for you, no matter what.

Jeremiah demonstrated in part what Jesus Christ demonstrated in full. Throughout our history as Christians, we have appropriated the songs of the suffering servant from Isaiah as being a perfect description of Christ. He had no form or comeliness that we should desire him. He was a man of sorrows. We esteemed him stricken by God, and so on. He was bruised for us. He bore our iniquities. Jesus took our suffering as though it were his own suffering and transformed it.

If you want to see creative suffering, start with Jesus. If you want to discover the power of creative crying, go to Jesus outside the tomb of his friend Lazarus. Through his tears came the cry of command, "Lazarus, come forth." Come forth out of death into life. See the power of death itself defeated. I believe that Jesus tears and his loud command were holding hands outside the tomb enclosing a man already dead and buried for four days. The tears of Jesus have great power because they are fueled by great love.

Jeremiah wept over the fate of Jerusalem. So did Jesus. In both times separated by several centuries, it was the time for crying. In both times, destruction came upon the city. In both times the destruction had begun long before the stones and bricks and buildings were destroyed. The destruction began in the hearts of

A Fellowship of Cracked Pots

those who lived there and who did not know when it was time to cry. They didn't know that godly sorrow should lead to repentance. They chose instead to fix a fake smile upon their faces and erect fake gods in their midst, gods who could neither heal or help or deliver when times get rough. They made a deal with the devil to go along so as to get along, trying to avoid the conflict between flesh and Spirit, between the kingdoms of this world and the Kingdom of God, between their self wills and the Will of God. It didn't work then. It doesn't work now. There is a time to laugh and a time to cry.

We men have been ruthlessly taught that big boys don't cry. Well, big boys, you'd better learn how. There is a time to cry. There are things in this world that if they don't break your heart, you have heart disease. God promised that in the New Covenant, he would remove our hearts of stone and put within us a heart of flesh, a heart that is working, is energetic, and is capable of being guided by the Spirit and broken by the world. David wrote in Psalm 51, "A broken and contrite heart O God thou wilt not despise."

When it comes time to cry, will you give your heart to the creative ministry of tears? In the end perhaps it will be our tears that water the spiritual dry ground around us and cause flowers of hope and healing and justice and righteousness to bloom in abundance. When it is time to cry, by all means, CRY!

Crumb Dog Millionaire

The Spirit inspired artistry of the Gospel writers is truly breathtaking. The way they tell the story of Jesus, teaching profound theology simply by putting things in context and particular sequence is wonderful.

Today's story about the Canaanite woman pleading with Jesus on behalf of her demon possessed daughter comes hot on the heels of one of Jesus' many sparring matches with the Scribes and the Pharisees recorded earlier in this 15th chapter. They'd come at Jesus with an accusatory tirade about his disciples eating food with unwashed hands. This was not due to a concern about germs or personal hygiene or public health. This was a squabble about the holiness code. "You and your crowd are not kosher. You are violating the rules and regulations of our religious law." That's what this was about.

Jesus rebuked their devotion to the law as though it was a matter of exterior observance rather than a matter of the heart. "What goes into the mouth is not important," said Jesus, "it's what comes out of the heart through the mouth that determines what is either clean or unclean." Jesus was so blunt that even the disciples were uneasy with how he had offended the religious leaders. Too bad for them. Deal with it.

With that as a backdrop Jesus heads off to Tyre and Sidon, to Canaanite country. This is tantamount to Bebe Netanyahu taking a little summer vacation in Gaza City. The Canaanites embodied everything anti-Israel from religion to geo-politics. It appears that what you read in the news today is nothing new. Is the implication that Jesus would rather be among the rank heathens than among the people who dressed up like they loved God but in their hearts, they were as far away as the Canaanites, maybe farther? Perhaps. Matthew says nothing directly about why Jesus went there but he relays a very telling story about what happened when he did.

Jesus was straightaway confronted by a Canaanite woman [two strikes already: wrong ethnicity, wrong gender] who had a demon possessed daughter. And this outsider addressed Jesus with ten times more respect than the people he was sent to, his own people. "Have mercy on me, Lord, Son of David. My daughter is tormented by a demon."

We will soon see that in this woman, Jesus has met his match, more so than he did from all the scribes and Pharisees the religious establishment could throw at him. She shouted at him with boldness born of desperation. She was a mother fighting for the life of her daughter against the forces of evil. With one brash cry, she touched the very heart of Jesus' vocation. His mission was ultimately to defeat the forces of hell and set human captives free. He came to demonstrate the triumph of the mercy of God.

This frantic woman, this mother of a tormented daughter refused to behave like an outsider. She called Jesus Lord, his title of divine authority. She called him Son of David, a title that in Israel conveyed strong messianic overtones. She was saying in effect in the face of exclusive Israel, "Your Messiah is my Messiah too!"

Jesus was for a moment speechless. The disciples fell into their stock answer when confronted by things they either felt unequipped to deal with or when they were pulled outside of their comfort zone. They knew what to do and they were not reticent to give Jesus advice just as they did when confronted by 5000 people with no food: "Send her away, for she keeps shouting at us." There it is again, their pet solution: "Send her away."

We can't blame them too harshly, or we shouldn't. Importunate, needy people can be so annoying, can't they? They always want something from you. They need food, they want money for gas or for a bus ticket or for a place to stay. They promise to pay you back but they never do. They show you some form of identification to prove they are not an outsider, not really. Here's my license, here's my social security card, here's my prescription. They confront us with a decision. Will we try to help or will we send them away? It's uncomfortable at best.

Confronted by this woman, Jesus was silent. He didn't say a word. What was going on inside his head? Some scholars believe that this was a moment of redefinition for Jesus of his own vocation. Jesus finally spoke out, "I was sent to the lost sheep of the house of Israel." In other words, at least for now, I must stay focused. But in this encounter, in this very moment with this female outsider from the enemy camp, were the parameters of Jesus' mission being expanded?

Some people erroneously think of Jesus from the manger onward as God in a human costume, as being all knowing and all seeing from the moment he was born. That makes no sense to me. Some with whom I agree see Jesus experiencing an ever-expanding awareness of what he was doing here and how and why, just like the rest of us thorough going human beings. He truly became one of us, like us in every respect except without sin. Just like us, Jesus experienced the life lived with God as an ever-unfolding saga of divine guidance and appointment to ministry. So, he wrestled in Gethsemane to be sure he was in God's will. He wrestled right up to the cross itself where we hear him cry, "My God, my God, why have you forsaken me?" Was that a true cry of anguish there on Good Friday, or do you think Jesus was just play acting for the crowd?

A Fellowship of Cracked Pots

In this encounter with the Canaanite woman, if they had been playing chess she would have at this point said, "Check," which means unless you figure out how to escape I'm going to take your king on the next move. Her cry became even more intimate and more direct, "Lord, help me." Notice how love has bound the mother to her daughter so tightly so that to help one was the same as helping the other.

This is why parents then and now pray with such fervor. We pray because our hearts are deeply invested in the health and wellbeing of our children. What hurts them wounds us. The bond between a mother and her child is that tight and that deep. And this wise and desperate mother was making a direct request as one who was rightly a child of Israel's God also. How could Jesus refuse her and stay true to his own nature and his own heart?

Jesus had one move left. "It is not fair to take the children's food and throw it to the dogs." It was a deft maneuver but not perfect, not perfect that is unless if down deep in his heart everything was reaching out in her direction. You see, Jesus used the Greek word for house dogs, not the usual term for wild, street dogs that could be mean and dangerous. The Jews used that more harsh term for Gentiles to indicate that they lived outside the realm of God's beneficent care and saving grace. Jesus used the kinder word for dogs, the one used for family pets. You dog lovers will know exactly what this means.

She saw her opening. He'd let her in like a stray about to be adopted. He might as well have placed a bowl of milk and some dog yummies on the floor in front of her. And she knew what to do with her next move. "Yes, Lord, yet even the dogs eat the crumbs that fall from their masters' table." Checkmate!

While those back in Israel were dickering, and obsessing about how much Jesus was breaking their religious rules and violating their moral taboos, this woman was equating exorcising demons as being akin to mere crumbs. Jesus had more power in his little finger to frustrate and defeat the powers of evil than all the practitioners of religion put together, Jew or Gentile. She wasn't just desperate; she was filled with faith and confidence. She knew her only hope was in Jesus and she went for him like a mother bear defending her cub.

Jesus marveled at her faith. And he found her faith irresistible. "Woman, great is your faith (exclamation point)! Let it be done for you as you wish." And it was. Her daughter was healed instantly. And so was this mother's heart.

Stepping back for a moment from these very individual and personal details, let's gather up the theological import of this story. The call upon Israel as it can be traced through God's covenant with Abraham was that Israel would be the fountainhead of God's blessings to all the peoples of the earth. They were failing in that mission. It seems as though Jesus initially saw his mission as to re-engage Israel's vocation by recalling them to their original ministry given to them by God. But the more they refused, the more the revelation of the Gospel began to burst at the seams of the too narrow perspective which saw Israel inside and everyone else outside and in no way worthy of God's attention. That God's love was intended to redeem the whole world, I believe Jesus knew from early on. But maybe how it so rapidly began to overflow the banks of the river of religion surprised even him.

In any event, overflow it did and continues to do to this day. And the river will continue to get deeper and wider as we draw ever closer to that day when Jesus comes to make all things new and to finally deliver every single one of us who are tormented by the demons of this world and of the pit of hell itself into the healing and the freedom always intended for us by God.

John sums it up so well in the very last chapter of our Bible in Revelation 22: "Then the angel showed me the river of the water of life, bright as crystal, flowing from the throne of God and of the Lamb through the middle of the street of the city. On either side of the river is the tree of life with its twelve kinds of fruit, producing its fruit each month; and the leaves of the tree are for the healing of the nations. Nothing accursed will be found there anymore. But the throne of God and of the Lamb will be in it, and his servants will worship him; they will see his face, and his name will be on their foreheads. And there will be no more night; they need no light of lamp or sun, for the Lord God will be their light, and they will reign forever and ever."

What begins as a few crumbs from the Masters' table will multiply until all the nations of the earth will be gathered into God's presence for healing and for eternal life. I'd say that makes of each one of us a crumb dog millionaire.

Demons in Worship

It's been several years ago now since I almost lost Jean. If you were around then you'll remember that she had a perforated appendix. It happened just days after we returned from the Johnsonburg retreat. She was in misery all night long. The next day we went to our family doctor, who of course couldn't see her until almost noon. He diagnosed appendicitis and sent us off to Cooper Hospital. I called our brother Jim who is a surgeon there and said, "Hey, we're headed down to the emergency department at your place." To make a long story short, we were camped in a hallway, hour upon hour with no relief in sight. Finally, I called Jim and said, "I don't know how close to death you need to be to be seen here, but things are really bad." A short time later, Jim showed up and I could hear the riot act being read to some folks down the hall. Things began to happen fast after that. It was a close call, way beyond too close for comfort, but all came out well in the end because I knew someone who had authority to make a difference. And every time I see Jim, gratitude for him wells up inside my soul.

Authority is like that. When things need to change, authority to make it happen is what is needed. When people long for truth, it takes someone with authority, someone who is not just guessing but who has genuine insight to deliver. When the creation goes awry under its own weight of sin and disease, what is needed is someone with enough clout to set things right. When people find themselves in the grip of one sort of bondage or another, whether the chains of their captivity have been forged out of the fires of their own foolish choices or they've been singled out for torment by demons from hell, what is needed is someone with strong enough authority to command their release.

A Fellowship of Cracked Pots

Our text from Mark this morning is only 8 verses long, but I went back and read all of chapter 1 because something caught my eye and I wanted to check it out. That something was one word: immediately. Mark has a brief introduction, tersely describes John the Baptist's ministry, and then gets right to the point of Jesus' baptism. With that, he puts me in mind of a little kid who has been down the street, around the corner, and who has just witnessed a robbery in progress at the local store, with police arriving, sirens wailing, who then make the arrest after blazing gunfire, wrestling the thief to the ground and slapping the handcuffs on him. So, the child rushes home, bursts through the door and breathlessly says, "Mom! Dad! You'll never guess what I just saw!"

Beginning with verse 9 and reading through the end of the chapter at verse 45, in 36 short verses, the word immediately is used 9 times, and just for a little variety in verse 28, Mark substitutes "at once". What's all the excitement about anyway? I want to focus in on our actual text in a minute, but let me give you a quick overview of all the excitement.

Jesus was baptized with water, with John's baptism for repentance, even though he was without sin and needed no repentance. Immediately the Holy Spirit descended, alit, and remained upon Jesus. Eyes of faith saw it happen. Believers later came to understand that this was the start of a brand new spiritual day. The Spirit's descent upon Jesus marked a crucial turning point in human spiritual life.

Then immediately, that same Holy Spirit drove Jesus up into the wilderness where he had his intense power encounter with his nemesis and our arch enemy, the devil himself.

After those victories over every temptation, Jesus took a stroll along the lake, immediately calling disciples who immediately left all they'd ever known, family, friends, and livelihoods to follow Jesus. We hear of no hesitation. Immediately, Jesus took his authority to the synagogue and began to teach. Then there was another power encounter and Jesus commanded deliverance for a poor soul [we'll return to him in a minute] and after being convulsed he was set free.

Then, immediately, Simon's sick mother in law was brought to Jesus and he healed her. Then a leper besought Jesus for cleansing and healing, and immediately he was made clean indeed! Calm down Mark. Take a deep breath.

Authority. For most of us whose mother tongue is rebellion, even the word authority looks like a red flag waving. One reason for this is that we have confused true authority with authoritarianism. The authoritarian is focused upon himself, what he wants, needs, and expects. She couldn't care less what your needs, wants, and expectations might be. When the authoritarian says, "Jump," our proper response is expected to be, "How high?" The authoritarian loves the old saw that some of us grew up with, "Don't do as I do; do as I say." Authoritarianism is the proper breeding ground for rebellion, whether it is overt if sufficient strength can be mustered, or passively aggressive when forced to go underground because the power differential is too great. So, whether we end up with overt hostility or sneaky deceit, relationships suffer.

The person with true authority is much different. Richard Rohr calls them light bulb people, people who give out energy rather than drain it from you. We've all known people who sucked us dry just being around them. Rohr says that most creative and alive people are not perfect. They have known their share of struggles and mistakes, but gained their inner authority by cooperating with grace, strength, and mercy. They take and give from an Unlimited Source.

Personal authority is rooted in personal experience. Recall the story of Jesus meeting the Samaritan woman at the well in John 4 when she attempted to dodge his authority by engaging in an abstract discussion about worship. Jesus came right to the point: "You Samaritans worship what you do not know, we testify about what we do know, for salvation is from the Jews." Her instinct to turn the discussion to the topic of worship as a way to mask her inner desolation was clever and creative and would have been successful if Jesus had lacked the authority he in fact embodied. She could have hidden in theological speculation all day long. She could have argued over whose mountain was the right mountain upon which to draw near to God. But real authority has a way of cutting away the underbrush and bringing the truth to light. Jesus taught her that true worship wasn't about climbing the right mountain; it was about approaching God with a true heart.

So, in our text today Jesus arrived in Capernaum on the Sabbath and immediately went to the synagogue and began to teach. And what teaching it was! It was entirely different from what the people were used to. They were used to someone standing up, reading scripture, and then ruminating about its meaning by appealing to their traditions, perhaps quoting a famous rabbi or two to shore up their opinions. There probably was a good bit of "on the one hand, but on the other hand" stuff, but certainly no "but I say to you" declarations. Jesus was so different. He was so strong that he flushed even demons out of hiding.

Have you ever gone to a worship service where the preaching lacked power and authority, where the sermon was just a series of cute stories linked together like a string of cheap beads? Or maybe the sermon tried so hard to be relevant that it majored on current events, or politics, or cultural trends but never proclaimed the majesty of Christ? My Uncle John once warned me as I started out on my own pulpit ministry: "No one wants to hear the preacher chasing the Jews around Jerusalem." He was not being anti-Semitic. I am certain he meant that the proclamation of the Gospel needs to be more than a biblical history lesson. People want the question, "So what?" to be answered. People need to know what you deeply know and they need to know how it applies to their lives.

Kierkegaard said that Christianity is an existence communication. Our faith and our testimony and our teaching must, if it is to have authority, spring up out of the quality of our discipleship, out of the very soil in which our lives are rooted and grounded. How shall we preach Christ if we have no personal knowledge of Christ? Unless the relationship is vital, the words of our speech will give no life to anyone.

Have you ever noticed that the words authentic and authenticity are closely related to authority? With spiritual authority there is no pretense, no role playing, no putting on airs, and no hypocrisy. With full authority and without a trace of arrogance or pride, Jesus declared, "I am the Way, and the Truth, and the Life. No one comes to the Father but by me." He also said things like, "You will know the truth and the truth will set you free."

When Jesus taught, as one who had authority, the people marveled and the demons trembled. In our story today, the demons were hiding in church, deep inside the soul of some poor man. He most likely didn't even know they were there. He probably thought he had his own hang-ups and some unresolved guilt but did not suspect demonic influence within. He was probably unaware of how bound up he was. He probably had a vague sense that he needed to remain hidden, afraid that if his fellow church members saw him for who he really was he would be rejected by all. Maybe he harbored a secret shame. Maybe he had an abiding sense of unworthiness. Maybe he'd learned how to appear religious and to wear his piety just like the others in church as a mask for his true heart condition. The darkness seems like your friend when your agenda is to stay hidden.

But Jesus is the ultimate light bulb person. And in the light of his teaching truth so directly and powerfully, the demons in the man could no longer contain themselves. "We know who you are, the Holy One of God. What do you want here? Have you come to destroy us?" To which Jesus said, "Shut up!" Jesus wasn't about to accept demonic worship. Their words were true but their hearts were false. Such worship is unacceptable to God whether they come from mouths either human or demonic. The demons had such a deep hold on this poor man that even in their releasing him, he was thrown into convulsions. And then they were gone. And then the man was set free, free to worship the Lord in Spirit and in truth.

Friends, Jesus came into the world of fallen human beings, Jesus came into the synagogues in the days of his earthly ministry, and Jesus comes into the Church in the power of the Holy Spirit today with full authority to save sinners. Jesus has the power to set the captives free. Jesus came and still comes to apply all the authority of heaven's throne to defeat the devil and his demons and to defeat death itself. His teaching is inspired. His healings are miraculous. His compassion is over all. His kindness and his mercy are resplendent with the Glory of God. Jesus has come to set all of us free from the powers that bind us and torment us and keep us hiding, even in Church, perhaps most pathetically and especially in Church, so that our worship will be banal and uninspired.

No flesh will be crucified in such worship. The highest aspiration of worship in the flesh is the desire to hear something interesting and to be entertained. Real transformation is not on the menu. Worship in Spirit and in Truth is vastly different. God comes continuously to set the captives free, to open blind eyes and prison doors.

Immediately after the benediction that day, Jesus' fame began to spread like wildfire in the entire surrounding region. The Jews, the Baptists, the Methodists, the Catholics, even the Presbyterians ran out and excitedly told any who would listen, "You'll never believe what happened in Church today. It was amazing. Let me tell you what Jesus did. Let me take you to meet him. He is truly amazing. He teaches like he knows what he's talking about. We've never heard anything like it. He speaks the truth directly with such power that it makes perfect sense to us. And we are filled with energy and joy and hope. And our old fears and worries just seem to waste away in his presence. Come and see for yourself."

Friends, now is the acceptable time. Today is the day of salvation. Please open your heart to the authority of the Risen Christ. You will never be sorry. In fact, you'll be more than glad you did.

Driving with No Brakes and No Reverse

I lived in rural Arkansas for a year. Our property was five miles from a paved road and ten miles from the town of Salem. We were surrounded by a 14,000-acre cattle ranch called The Lazy M owned by some rich Texan. On the way to our place, there was a small farmstead owned by the Birch family who I'm guessing would qualify as rural poor people. They lived in a small run down house surrounded by the usual junk like old washing machines and carcasses of cars and tractors and trucks scattered around. There was also a population of assorted animals running about including chickens, cats, and dogs of many genetic mixtures. None looked that well fed, but I guess they survived.

I bought my first truck there in Arkansas, a '57 Chevy half ton pickup. The guy who sold it to me said it was a good old truck, a steal at $250. Then the brakes went bad. I could still get them to work if I pumped the brake pedal about eight times. Later I would learn how to fix them myself and how to bleed the lines to get air out of them, sort of like a nurse clearing an IV.

One day while passing the Birch place, one of their scruffy dogs chased me, jumped in front of the truck, and I ran over him, killing him instantly. I stopped, went to the house and told them about it. They didn't seem upset at all. He was a stray who had recently wandered in and they really didn't want him anyway. I still felt terrible. I guess it's still a memory that evokes regret in me. Even in extreme rural areas, it's still irresponsible to drive with bad brakes.

I also remember a friend who had a car with a transmission that no longer had reverse. That required some forethought when doing things like parking. If you wanted to back up, you had to get out and push. Now I know you didn't come here to hear some old codger tell truck and car stories and to reminisce about how things used to be. And I didn't come here to tell you about all that either. It's just what I thought of when I thought about Jesus in the text today.

The Pharisees wanted Jesus to throw on the brakes, put it in reverse, and get out of their neighborhood. They were constantly trying to slow him down and to push him back from his mission. To them, Jesus was nothing more than a dangerous blasphemer who was trying to lead people astray by getting them out from under their Pharisaic thumbs. They figured a threat about Herod's evil intentions would do the trick nicely.

If you want to do an interesting little study, Google Herod. You'll see that this Herod named Antipas was the son of Herod the Great, the rebuilder of the Jerusalem temple. Herod the Great was the first of a four-generation dynasty of rulers whom the Romans permitted to govern various parts of the Holy Land. Herod the Great was the vicious tyrant who tried to trick the Magi who came looking for the new born king of the Jews. It was Herod who tried to find Jesus as an infant and snuff out his young life. Failing that, in a furious and paranoid rage, he had all the male infants less than two year's old slain in and around Bethlehem. Caesar was reputed to have said it was better to be Herod's dog than his son, because he actually killed two of his boys whom he suspected of having designs upon the throne of dear old dad.

After his death, Herod the Great's son, Herod Antipas ruled one quarter of his father's region after a big family squabble between him and some of his brothers each of whom felt entitled to the succession to be ruler. They traveled to Rome to appeal to Caesar about their inheritance. Caesar ruled that Herod Antipas could keep his one quarter of the reign. That's why he was known as Herod the tetrarch, because of the one quarter deal.

Along the way, Herod Antipas visited his stepbrother, fell in love with his wife, and eventually took her for himself. This is where John the Baptist got involved, shouting loudly that incest was not best, that Herod was in serious trouble with God. John eventually lost his head in the deal because Herod couldn't control his own lust, which is a story for another sermon.

The point is, Jesus was being reminded, shall we say threatened by these Pharisees, with the danger of a malicious ruler who was capable of gross violence with no concern for justice whatsoever. "Hit the brakes Jesus! Put it in reverse and get out of here!" To which Jesus response was, "Tell that fox to go get a life. He has no power over me at all. I will be destroyed, but not by him. I have my own destiny, destination, and timetable. And it won't be long now."

The thing I admire so much about Jesus, one of the things, is that no one ever was able to intimidate him. He seemed to have no brakes and no reverse. He came for the particular purpose of laying down his life for sinners and nothing could stand in his way. In fact, he had the ability to make even his enemies serve his purpose and advance his mission. And on top of all that, he had such a tender heart, full of compassion, mercy, and grace, that he even lamented over those most dedicated to his destruction. And all that animosity was focused in the city which was the most religious of all cities, Jerusalem.

Jerusalem, the site of the holy temple of the living God. Jerusalem, the destination of hundreds of thousands of pilgrims who went up to worship there every year. Jerusalem, the City of David and Solomon, of Isaiah and Jeremiah and Ezekiel. Jerusalem: the very name implies shalom, the peace of God, the total wellbeing that comes from following God's Word and plan and seeking God's righteousness.

But Jesus had a different description of the Holy City. Jesus lamented that Jerusalem was the city famous for killing the prophets and stoning those who are sent to her. Even a cursory reading of the Gospels reveals that nearly all of Jesus' arguments and experiences of resistance and rejection came from the most religious people. He expressed little interest in confronting the Romans (what kind of Messiah is he anyway?). He seemed most at home when hanging around with sinners who needed grace and outcasts who needed acceptance, and broken people with all kinds of wounds who needed to be healed.

From the very outset of his ministry we see that Jesus is no ladder climber. Satan tried to seduce him with pride and power and religious influence and Jesus refused to play ball. Jesus promised living water to those who would come to him in faith, and like common water, living water seems always to seek the lowest level, and down there in the dumps of existence to refresh, renew, and even resurrect people to new life.

Jesus lamented over the spiritually proud, self-righteous religiously serious denizens of both synagogue and temple. He used the image of a mother hen who longs to gather her chicks under her wings when danger is near. If I'm remembering my chicken knowledge properly, a mother hen has a certain cluck that her chicks instantly respond to by running for cover under her wings. Maybe chickens and their babies are not as dumb as they look. And maybe uptight religious types are not as smart as they pretend to be. In fact, maybe they are dumber than baby chickens.

In those days, the religious leaders had a real pride problem. They refused, over and over again in many a generation to refuse to heed God's call. If God said return to me, they'd argue that they were already close to God. They claimed to understand the Law of God while at the same time trivializing its demands, like tithing herbs and ignoring deeds of compassion and mercy. If God said repent, they would take refuge in how good they already were. That call would lead them to point their fingers at others who needed repentance more than they did. They were like Presbyterians who hear the word powerfully proclaimed and sit in the pew wishing Uncle Joe or teenaged rebels Jack and Jill were here to hear it. It's a time proven, threadbare strategy to dodge the convicting power of the Holy Spirit. You might say people who do that in any generation are dumb clucks; you might say that. I'm too much of a diplomatic preacher to risk such labeling.

It literally broke Jesus' heart to have to say to these religious elites, "Behold, your house is forsaken." In other words, you will keep coming to what you call worship, hoping to find God in your midst like in the days of old from Genesis or Exodus, or from the glory days of King David and King Solomon, or even the days of renewal as were the days of Nehemiah, but unlike them, you will not find God. Your hearts are too far from me. Your house is forsaken.

When you think about it, any religious institution, whether a congregation or a whole denomination, which begins to take God for granted and fails to stay in touch with the head, Jesus Christ, also begins to first flounder and then shrink and die. The ability to see Jesus is lost. Jesus said to those Pharisees so long ago, you will not see me until you say, "Blessed is he who comes in the name of the Lord." And the words are not a magic formula either. They shouted them on Palm Sunday and look what happened just five days later. The shouts became, "Crucify, crucify him."

What blesses Jesus and gives us eyes to see and ears to hear and wills to respond with obedience is a heart contrite, broken, and open to the indwelling presence of Jesus' Spirit. Jesus wants us to implant the deepest part of his nature into the deepest recesses of your nature and mine. It is the indwelling of the Holy Spirit that reverses the god forsakenness that we experience due to sin. The Holy Spirit regenerates within us the love of God and God loves us to life, abundant life here and eternal life forever.

Have you opened your heart to Christ? Was it open once, but under the seductions and powers of the world, has it slowly hardened or become indifferent to the things of the Spirit. I urge you, be at least as smart as a baby chicken. Don't be a dumb cluck. The dangers are real in this world. Run to Jesus for the covering, hovering, protective presence of the living God. God is your refuge and strength!

Endurance

It's tempting to read this and other similar texts as "end of the world" descriptions. They may be that but let's step back from the ultimate end for a moment and try to see what else is here.

We find Jesus and twelve men, called to be disciples, who left everything to follow Jesus. They've come to believe that he is the long-awaited Messiah promised to Israel. Now they're on the inside, the very inner circle. It dawns on them that they have a front row seat. Jesus has told them that they will reign with him. They've seen mighty signs and wonders pointing to glory, God's glory and Jesus' victory. And they thought they could begin to see the outlines of that glory. Jesus has overcome every obstacle placed in his path. He has bested every opponent in his ministry. Walking through the spiritual center of Israel on the streets of old Jerusalem stars filled their eyes. They weren't in Nazareth anymore, or Capernaum, or any other backwater Galilean village. This was God's Holy City, the appointed location for the abode of the Glory of the Living God. And they figured they were about to ascend to the heights and sit upon thrones next to Jesus Messiah. Who could find fault with their wide-eyed wonder?

Well, Jesus. His words must have felt like a slap in the face, or a kick to their spiritual stomachs, or like a bucket of cold reality water dousing their fantasy world. What they longed for may not be that much different from what we long for, a time where justice would run down like waters and righteousness like an ever-flowing stream. Who among us doesn't want to hasten the time when every tear will be wiped from our eyes, when even death will be no more, a time when the former things will have passed away? There is not a thing wrong with all such desires. But there is no promised shortcut to the Promised Land. We must all pass through the wilderness first.

"Look Master, all these marvelous stones!"

"There will soon come a time when not one of these stones will be left standing. It's all coming down. Destruction is imminent. Take care not to get caught up adoring things that won't last!"

Jesus is talking to disciples, to learners, to people like us. He is saying, "Don't send your adoration in the wrong direction. Don't invest your heart's devotion and energy in things that will not last. Don't store up treasures where moth and rust devour. Resist false assumptions and wrong conclusions. The time is coming when you will see the mighty stones of the human aspiration to go your own way with or without God come tumbling down." To that teaching, the learners ask the obvious question: "When?"

When will the time come? They are still scrambling to stay in control. We humans like to know what time it is and what is about to happen so we can plan ahead for our survival. Jesus never answers the question. He simply gives a hair-raising description of what will take place before that time.

Making the list of what to expect is just about everything you and I might find on our list of things to fear. Have you ever taken the time to name your fears? Some are afraid to die. Some are afraid to get sick, or old, or that they won't have enough money to get them from cradle to grave. Some are obsessed with what other people think of them. My late mentor Dr. Loder used to share the words of one of his counselees, "I hope I die before I ruin my reputation." Some are afraid to be alone. Some are afraid not to be alone. Some are afraid of flying too high, others are afraid of sinking too deep into an inescapable depression. Some are afraid to lose control, are terrified of words like surrender. What scares you? The possibilities are endless.

We've all just come through almost two years of electioneering by people who wanted to become president. Most of us want to go take a long shower to try to wipe all the political scum off of our skin. We've all been schooled in what to fear and whom to hate. As I write this the day before the national election, I already know that come Sunday (today), half of us will be convinced that all hope is gone, while the other half will still dare to hope, even if just a little, that all is not lost. The politicians have played on our fears like skilled harpists of the Apocalypse.

I thank God I still remember the words of the great hymn, The Solid Rock that says, "My hope is built on nothing less than Jesus' blood and righteousness. I dare not trust the sweetest frame, but wholly lean on Jesus' name. On Christ the solid rock I stand; all other ground is sinking sand; all other ground is sinking sand."

Jesus gives us a list of things we might expect to encounter before the answer to "when?" becomes "now." Expect spiritual imposters to show up, religious charlatans who will play upon your spiritual desires to gain an ungodly advantage over you. They'll play on your fears, your hopes and your expectations to lead you astray. And once they knock you off course, they will exploit you for their own gain. Don't go after them. Don't go out. Don't follow them.

You will see wars, and hear rumors of wars, and insurrections. You will hear of all kinds of natural disasters and human tragedies. They will be splashed all over the news. You will have trouble escaping the constant barrage of fearful reports of devastations. There will even be cosmic signs in the heavens.

Jesus continues as if what he has warned about is not yet enough. Even before that you will be arrested and persecuted. The religious people will question your orthodoxy. Prisons will be built to take away your freedom. You'll be called into court to give an account of yourselves before governors and kings. You'll be in so deep you won't know what to say or how even to defend yourselves (but don't worry Jesus promises, I'll tell you what to say and I will give you an unbeatable wisdom). You'll be betrayed by those closest to you, by even family and best friends. You'll be hated because of my name, because you dare to identify with me. Oh yes, and I almost forgot to mention, some of you will be put to death. But don't worry, not a hair of your head will perish. Jesus seems to think it takes a great deal to get the stars out of disciples' eyes.

Talk about a church growth strategy! I wonder if we ran an ad in the Courier Post urging people to come be a part of such glorious prospects if even one person would come near. I recently read a story in a devotional by Richard Rohr. An angel was walking down the street with a torch and a bucket of water. A woman happened along and asked, "What are you doing with the torch and the bucket?" And the angel replied, "With the torch I am going to set fire to all the mansions of heaven, and with the bucket I am going to extinguish the fires of hell. Then we shall see who really loves God."

If you remove all the promise of reward and all the threat of punishment, what is left? For one thing, you have created the possibility of real love. If we love the way God loves, it is neither for gaining reward nor for avoiding punishment. Love is its own reward. And sometimes love is experienced much like a punishment when it goes unrequited. To have love to give and no one willing to receive it is agonizing. The Cross of Christ illustrates the cost all too well. The one who hangs there as the perfect embodiment of God's love is brutally rejected. The pain is ugly and all too real.

I don't believe Jesus' main didactic aim in this and other warning passages is to scare people away. He is teaching to prepare the people he loves. He is being brutally honest about how things are and how they will be for quite some time, during the time before the end. His warnings are born of love. The watchword for this season is endurance. By your endurance, you will gain your souls. Endurance through trials carries with it transformational power. Endurance teaches you more valuable things than all the instant gratification in the world could ever do.

Walking the Camino, I saw many beautiful churches, adorned inside with elaborate statuary covered in gold. I went into some magnificent cathedrals, in Burgos, in Leon, and in Santiago. But where I really learned most about myself and about God was out on the open road, where my feet hurt and my muscles ached, and where the miles crept by, sometimes with agonizing slowness. It was out there, in the spaces between the beautiful churches, in the walking through a great wide open, that I came closest to God. It was in the midst of the difficulty, beset with sore feet and aching muscles and longing for my next place to lay my head that I most experienced the sustaining power of my God. I got what I needed. It was there that I gained my soul more deeply than ever before.

So here we all are gathered in our beautiful sanctuary. We come to be encouraged, to be loved and cared for, and to find strength for the open road. Some of us have had major seasons calling for endurance of very difficult things. We come to hear the promises of God. We come so as not to forget the majesty of God. We come for hugs and outstretched hands and the open hearts of our fellows so as to mute the power of our aloneness.

Your soul is that part of you that has real depth. It is in your soul that the Holy Spirit works to deliver you from your fears and your unbelief. It is there where spiritual combat is most fierce. It is there you are made strong in the Lord.

Endurance is to faith as weight lifting is to muscle. Sooner or later, every one of us will enter the school of endurance. Sooner or later, God will use the demands of endurance to forge a soul in you that is well suited for eternal life, the quality of life that is yours and mine in Christ Jesus. When you come into the time of trial, look to Jesus, the pioneer and perfecter of your faith. Consider him who, for the glory set before him, endured the cross, disregarding its shame. Instead of asking when will the season of victory arrive, ask instead for the strength to endure whatever comes your way so that you might glorify God in your body.

Funeral Wrecker

The thing about Skink is he's not a real person. Skink is the nickname for the protagonist in a series of entertaining novels I've read who had been a hero in U.S. special ops. After his distinguished military service, he rose to be governor of Florida. Then one day, he couldn't take it anymore. He became fed up with all the corruption. He became outraged as land developers made shady deals so they could rape pristine stretches of beachfront and island real estate and turn them into condos and resorts. So, one day he walked away from it all. His only trusted contact in the world he left was an African American who was a Florida state trooper. No one else knew where he went or what happened to him.

Skink set up camp in the swamps of South Florida and lived off the land. From time to time, his adventures turned him into south Florida's version of Robin Hood. He would rescue everything from damsels in distress to parcels of precious wilderness under threat from greedy developers and their huge machines of construction destruction. One of Skink's methods of survival was the consumption of road kill. He couldn't stand to see good meat go to waste.

Like I said, Skink was not a real person. But the people we just read about were real people, even though they lived a long time ago. They had hopes, dreams, and expectations as real and numerous as any of us. They were people like the ones today who live in Pennsauken, Merchantville, Cherry Hill, or Camden. They loved their lives, their children, and their God. They labored to survive and they said their prayers. And they suffered just like any of us do who live here.

William Gaskill

Elijah was revered as one of Israel's greatest prophets. He lived and served the Lord at the time of King Ahab, one of Israel's most corrupt kings spiritually and politically. So, God instructed Elijah to command a three-year drought in the land and no rain fell. Like Skink, Elijah holed up in the wilderness, drank muddy water from the wadi, and fed on road kill provided by the local ravens. I don't know if you've ever seen what crows eat but let's just say if you went out to dinner you wouldn't order it.

When the wadi dried up, Elijah was directed to head for enemy territory, the land of Sidon, and cast his lots with a poor widow there. Talk about vulnerability; Elijah was forced to the edge of existence right along with all his fellow Israelites who were experiencing God's judgment.

What I find so fascinating about this story is not so much Elijah's obedience to God's command. I expect that from a prophet. And it's not so much God's judgments that come upon spiritual, moral, and political corruption. I expect that from a holy God. And it's not even so much the poor widow's willingness to share what she thought was her last meal she had hoarded for herself and her only son. Things had gotten so severe for her that one meal more or less no longer mattered much. It would do no good to prolong her misery, so why not take the chance on Israel's man of God. She had nothing much to lose by this point. And I'm not even astounded by the miraculous multiplication of grain and oil which sustained all three, the prophet, the widow and her son as the drought ground on and on. I already know our God is a God of miracles, well able to change water into wine and feed vast throngs of hungry people with a few loaves and fishes.

No, what I'm focused on is what happens when the child dies. Now the Bible has my undivided attention. I like what I consider to be the widow's justifiable outrage. She's mad at Elijah and at his

God. After all I've done for you, this is the thanks I get? Why did you prolong my life? Was it just so I could be forced to endure a mother's worst nightmare, the death of her only child?

I understand her anger. I get the force of her questions. And so does Elijah. The outsider and the insider, the Gentile widow and the great prophet of Israel, both have questions for God. As the insider, as the appointed representative who speaks for God, Elijah gets the honor of taking the case before God. Elijah took the corpse of the boy from the arms of his weeping, devastated mother, hauled him upstairs to the guest room and spread him out on his own bed. Then he talked to God. "O Lord, my God, have you brought calamity even upon the widow with whom I am staying, by killing her son?"

You could read this as a simple and dispassionate question, something like, "Is this part of the plan too Lord?", as though Elijah is being merely inquisitive about God's providence and plan. But I think that misses the point. Elijah is no bland, milquetoast preacher. I think even Elijah is offended at the price of judgment if it goes so far as to afflict a helpless woman who has offered all the help she could in deference to God and God's prophet. Elijah seems to me to be asking, "Is this who you really are God? Is this how you treat people?"

Any bereaved parent knows these questions intimately and intensely. So do prophets and pastors in all times. There is so much that goes on for which we lack the insight and understanding to interpret the meaning. We sometimes find ourselves mute before suffering; we know the questions but we have none of the answers.

At this point, Elijah makes the right move and it's not easy or obvious. He leaves behind his accusations of God and starts to pray. "O Lord, my God, let this child's life come into him again."

He prayed it once. Nothing happened. He prayed it twice. Still there were no signs of life. The prayer was still unanswered. He just kept on going, not willing to take "no" for an answer. His perseverance seemed to matter somehow. We have a saying, "The third time's the charm." The third time he prayed, life suddenly came back into the dead boy and he was alive again.

Jesus on the cross in the midst of unimaginable agony cried out to his Father, "My God, my God, why…?" Elijah too was talking directly: "O Lord, my God….!" Both make a statement of faith in the face of their greatest trials. Both men knew where to take their agony. Elijah prayed and prayed for life, and finally the God of life granted his petition. And one Gentile woman at the bottom of the social register even in her own land became a believer that day: "Now I know that you are a man of God, and that the word of the Lord in your mouth is truth."

Bread enough to survive didn't do it. Oil that refused run out didn't do it. The endless supply of necessities and luxuries were not enough to satisfy or comfort a mother's heart when the child died. When one of us loses a beloved child or someone else whom we dearly love, what to eat is not that important to us. Neither are all the old pleasures that used to take up so much of our emotional energy.

The only comfort that would do for the widow was the life of her son restored to her. And she got what she needed, and so did Elijah. They both got answered prayers. They both got renewed confidence in God. They both went to a deeper level of trust in God than they ever knew before. God is the author and sustainer of life. God is the Lord even over death. That day they both discovered a new depth to the love of God.

Fast forward quite a few hundred years to the time of Jesus. Elijah was so revered that the tradition was that he would return to be the forerunner and sign that the Messiah had come. Jesus told people that John the Baptist was the fulfillment of that expectation. When Jesus queried the disciples about whom people said he was, one of their answers was, "Some say you are Elijah."

Elijah did notable signs; so did Jesus. Elijah raised a boy from the dead; so did Jesus in our text from Luke 7. In Luke's account, there are no prayers recorded. We are told none of the details of the boy's death or the faith of his mother. She too is a broken-hearted widow from a small and insignificant village and the boy was her only son. Her son, in addition to being her beloved would have provided her with social security. Without him, life would become a grim affair of survival.

We're not supposed to read into Bible stories what's not there, but perhaps in this case we can safely surmise that the question is close at hand: "What kind of God do we have? How can God allow stuff like this to happen?" We can surmise this because those questions always seem to arise when a child is lost.

Jesus happened upon the funeral procession, the body being carried through the village streets amidst the loud cries and wailing of the mourners. Luke tells us, "When the Lord saw her he had compassion for her…" In that instant, Jesus revealed what kind of God we have. Our God is a God of compassion. Our God has a word to say, "Do not weep." Why? Because our God is a God of life. Our God combines compassion with the power to make a difference. In this instance, the child was restored to life. But that's not always how it works is it.

Jesus had a deeper work that he came to do. Everyone ever restored to life in the Bible stories where that happened, went on and lived, then later, died again. The Sidonian widow's son died. The widow from Nain's son died. Even Jesus' good friend Lazarus eventually had to go through it again: he too died. There are several more such stories in the Bible. Each person restored to life, eventually died.

Even Jesus died at the young age of 33, too young by our standards. His own mother stood at the foot of his cross and had her heart ripped open. These stories which we all get to live sooner or later seem gruesome.

But if we shift the focus to the deeper story about God and creation and sin and death and eternal life, we see that Jesus didn't just come to protect us from what Paul described as our slight momentary afflictions. Jesus came to obliterate our eternal afflictions by removing both sin and death from the fabric of God's good creation which has been infected from the first-time human beings decided they could go it alone without God. We were made for intimacy and love between us and our creator, an intimacy which was broken and lost with that decision to live independently. Jesus came as the repairer of the breech and to restore us to our originally intended glory.

So often, the miracle stories, the stories of exceptional compassion and lavish grace, spawn their own questions. The prodigal son's older brother gives them voice: "What about me?" he whines out in the back yard, refusing to go in to celebrate with the family. No doubt other parents were in the crowd that day, mothers and fathers who too had lost a child. What about me? What about us? Why did she get a miracle and we're here left with our broken hearts?

This story yields no answers nor does it try to do so. It simply says, Jesus had compassion upon her. Our God is compassionate, no matter what circumstances are ours to endure. It may not come to our full awareness until we enter fully into God's presence and there see the depth of God's love for each one of us. Until then, what can we do but pray and trust? We too need to learn to preface all of our "why" questions with the confession, "My God, my God...O Lord my God," because if we don't all we are left with is futile bitterness and abject despair, and God has much better in store for us than that. Jesus died to give us a living hope through the resurrection.

Get Your Ears On

Let's begin this morning with a little exercise. Stretch your hands out in front of you. Now slowly, being careful not to inadvertently slap the person next to you, raise them up and place your palms on the side of your head. Do you feel them? Those are your ears. God made those ears. They have many useful functions in our lives, but the most important purpose of your ears is to hear God with them through God's word. That's why the Bible is so important. That's why we have preachers (I know you've often wondered why we have preachers). Our ears are not the only way we can hear God. We can also hear God through our mind, through our conscience, or by the Holy Spirit bringing conviction deep inside applying it to what the Bible calls our heart.

Have you ever been perplexed by people like me who say things like, "The Lord said to me," and, "I was praying the other morning and the Lord told me to...", or "I was going the wrong way until God intervened and caused me to change direction"? My adult Christian life began for me in a profound experience of being addressed by God. It was intense and involved a sharp rebuke from the Lord. You can read about it in some detail in my book <u>Gold Mining in the Pit of Sorrow</u>. Not to bore you again with the gory details, God called me a liar and explained that I could be nothing else because I didn't have the truth in me. How did I know it was God? Because I would have been much more gentle with myself, that's why. God got my attention.

A few years later, I was a Christian man, not sure where I was going or what I was to do with my life other than work for a living when God addressed me again. It was Easter Sunday. This was nearly 40 years ago but my memory of it is still vivid in my mind. I was in worship at Narberth Presbyterian Church, seated on the left side of the sanctuary about eight rows from the front, closer to the stained-glass windows on the side than to the center aisle. Pastor George was no doubt waxing eloquent about the resurrection. I don't remember the sermon at all. But for some months I'd been wrestling with the Lord about a possible call upon my life to seek ordained ministry. What I remember was God saying to me directly as I was listening to the pastor, "You'll never be happy until you are doing that!" So, here I am. And I am happy!

I find the call stories in the Bible, of which there are very many, to be quite compelling. We just heard the account of the call of the young boy named Samuel to become a prophet in Israel. You'll remember that Samuel was Hannah's prayed for baby boy. She had promised God if God would take away her barrenness that the child who would come as the answer to her prayers would be handed over to God to serve the Lord all the days of his life.

When Samuel was born, Hannah kept him until he was weaned, then made good on her promise. Giving an only son to serve as priest before God on behalf of people; what an amazing concept. She took him up to the temple at Shiloh and handed him over to the priest named Eli to be raised up to be the servant of the Lord. Somehow Hannah understood, unlike so many people, that one should not make vows to God and then not keep them. I'm in awe nevertheless that she made good on her promise to let her child go. Eli took the boy and raised him and employed him in the religious duties of a priest.

To put it kindly, it doesn't sound like Eli was the perfect mentor. He sounds like a man who was just going through the religious motions. He had his own sons working with him in the priestly ministry and they were mishandling the sacrifices brought by the people and having illicit sex with the women who served at the temple. Eli knew it but failed to put a stop to it. The judgment of

God finally came upon him and on his house. This is the backdrop to verse 1 of I Samuel 3 which says, "Now the boy Samuel was ministering to the Lord under Eli. The word of the Lord was rare in those days; visions were not widespread."

In short, people were not hearing God's word and were not seeing the things of real importance, the things of God. Their religious leaders had religion, but it was empty. And as it always does, empty religion sooner or later leads people to treat spiritual things with contempt as did the sons of Eli, or at best lie slumbering near the temple in spiritual indifference while evil goes unchecked both inside and outside the church.

So, while Eli is in bed and Samuel has pulled the night shift in the temple, the voice of the Lord calls out to Samuel. The voice calls him by name. In case you don't know, this is how God does call each one of us, by name. God has a unique and complete knowledge of every one of our lives. With God, one size does not fit all. Every person is a custom model, a rare treasure in God's sight. Did you know or even suspect this about yourself?

If you double back to chapter 1, you'll see that when Hannah came to Eli's church and was pouring her heart out to the Lord in prayer, he thought she was drunk and rebuked her. When she said no, she was rather in deep prayer with the Lord; he dismissed her with a little religious bromide: "Go in peace; the God of Israel grant you the petition you have made of him." I came across a surprising little footnote in my study Bible that likened Eli's incomprehension with that of the bystanders on the first Christian Pentecost who said when they heard the people praying in tongues, "They are drunk. They're filled with new wine."

Let's say charitably that the natural man and woman tend to be a little dense when it comes to God's working, God's speaking, and

God's calling. God was nothing that night if not persistent. Finally, after three times, Eli recognized that God was calling upon the boy Samuel and gave him good counsel. Go back to the temple, when he calls, answer, and when he speaks, listen carefully to all God says.

May I ask you quite directly, when you set out to come to worship, do you bring with you the expectation that you are about to be addressed by God. And have you made up your mind that when you perceive God addressing you, you will give God your undivided attention as well as making a heartfelt, life engaging response to what you hear? It's important to notice that the Bible says that the Lord came and stood before Samuel, but what is recounted as most significant is not a vision but a message. It's not usually what the eye sees that counts most; it's what the ear hears and how the heart responds that is crucial.

You might think, "Well that's all fine. But God would never call a person like me. I'm too unimportant, or I have too many sins, or I have too much personal baggage weighing me down. Most people harbor something that they think disqualifies them from the divine call to be uniquely special in the work of God's kingdom. But it's not so. Can you imagine how different the world would be today if every single person ever born had given themselves over to God's purpose and plan and had boldly offered themselves and their particular gifts in service to God and God's world? It would be drastically different. It would be amazing. But let's not get lost is such a huge "what if." Let's simply apply it to ourselves: "What if, from this day forward, I respond to God's call. What if I go forth from here knowing I've been encountered, addressed, and given a mandate to live a new kind of life?"

Leaving Samuel who became great in his generation and zooming forward to Jesus' time when he was calling disciples, ask yourself what kind of people were being called. We don't see Jesus traveling up to Jerusalem to recruit the religious heavy-weights, the scholars and the priests. No, we see him down by the docks calling fishermen, in the market places calling tax collectors. We see him calling betrayers, deniers, and skeptics, and simple common people with their sins and shortcomings, their fears and doubts and lack of vision.

Paul, writing to the Corinthians, put it this way: "Consider your own call brothers and sisters: not many of you were wise by human standards, not many were powerful, not many were of noble birth. But God chose what is foolish in the world to shame the wise; God chose what is weak in the world to shame the strong; God chose what is low and despised in the world, things that are not, to reduce to nothing things that are, so that no one might boast in the presence of God." I Corinthians 1:26-29.

Any one of the named disciples could teach us a thing or two. I love to consider Nathanial. He's the one in today's Gospel reading who asks the cynical and acerbic question, "Can anything good come out of Nazareth?" Nathanial is sitting under a fig tree. It's not kosher to read the Bible too allegorically, but it is interesting that the fig tree was one of the symbols Israel adopted for herself. The fig tree is the one that's fruit is delicious and sweet and nutritious, just like Israel was supposed to be spiritually.

But it's not automatic. It wasn't in Eli's day, it wasn't in Nathanial's day, and it's certainly not true in our day. Spiritual life cannot be faked. It's more than a show or an exercise in churchy theater. Our encounters with the living God and God's call upon our lives are intense. They demand, as our great hymn "When I Survey the Wondrous Cross" says, "my life, my soul, my all."

Jesus says, "While you were under the fig tree, I saw you." I saw you when you were too cool for school. I saw every cynical bone in your body. I saw your superior attitude that convinced you you were "all that" because you hail from Bethsaida rather than Nazareth. And I saw something I like very much: there's no guile in you. You are not phony or fake. You tell it like it is and call it the way you see it. I like that in a man. Jesus confers upon cynical Nathanial not tongue clucking disapproval. I can well see a smile on Jesus' face and a twinkle in his eye as he wins Nathanial over so easily.

The text tells us that Jesus found Philip and said, "Follow me." Just a few words later, Philip finds his brother Nathanial and says, "We have found the Messiah." Who found who? Jesus finds us in such a respectful loving way that we are so built up that we think we made the discovery. But the truth of Grace is that we are sought and found before we ever find anything. We find Jesus because we have been found by him.

What I'm trying to say and what I want to convince you of today if at all possible is that your name is on God's lips, right now, in this world, in this, your one and only life. You are more precious to Jesus Christ than you can estimate, sum up, or calculate. How then shall we live, you and me, in response to this great Gospel truth? I commend the question to your thoughts, your reflection, and to your going forward from this moment.

Hearts and Treasures

Jesus said, "Do not be afraid, little flock, for it is your Father's good pleasure to give you the kingdom." And two verses later he said, "For where your treasure is, there your heart will be also." So, the other day, I was sitting on my deck with morning coffee mulling these things over.

I've been reading once again Annie Dillard's work, Pilgrim at Tinker Creek. I read her and other writers like her as a way to try and keep my eyes open. I've found that life in the modern world with all its noise, attractions, distractions, and seductions has a mind numbing, sight reducing, insight eclipsing impact on my soul and I suspect on your soul as well. I battle to keep awake and alive.

So, there I sat considering what has been given to me by my Father's good pleasure when it says that the gift is the kingdom. I began to just look around me, maybe not as insightfully as Annie Dillard at Tinker Creek. I was just Bill in Cherry Hill. I started out with what I could see and hear. I began to notice the large variety of plant life. I saw how the rising sun gradually illuminated the leaves of maples and sweet gums and Chinese lilacs, and bamboo, and each needle of the massive white pines, and the delicate lace of Japanese maples that came from seeds blown over from my neighbor's yard years ago.

And I heard the call of many birds, most of whose songs and squawks and chirps I have learned to identify over the years. Jean and I call the early morning cacophony the chirp fest. I like to think that before our little feathered friends go off on the daily round of scavenging for food, those bird brains are smart enough to know that the first order of each day is to praise God from whom all blessings flow. I've never heard a bird start the day by complaining, not even on Monday.

I looked at all the stuff surrounding me, tables and chairs made of metal and plastic, at the wood of the deck, in this case it is made of redwood. And I considered my house and yard and that all was surrounded by hundreds of other homes with whole families of people living there, each with a web of relationships, and so on and on and on. I thought of all the people who produced all these things I take for granted and all the trappings and benefits of civilization like electricity and plumbing, and don't forget air conditioning. Then there is all the rest of the stuff that is there to see or take for granted as you choose.

Annie Dillard noted that in one square foot of top soil there are well over 1,350 life forms! I saw this for myself the other day when I was cutting the lawn. I moved an inverted trash can in order to mow, and there inside were thousands of little ants with thousands of little eggs. I moved another and there scurried away thousand leggers and surprised snails and a myriad of other creepy crawlers panicked by the sudden burst of light upon their hiding place.

In theological terms, these observations would come under the section entitled "The Knowledge of God the Creator" as it did in Calvin's <u>Institutes of the Christian Religion.</u> And we haven't even considered the night sky filled with its constellations and infinite expanse. No wonder the Psalmist exclaimed in Psalm 8: O Lord our Lord, how majestic is your name in all the earth.... When I look at your heaven, the work of your fingers, the moon and the stars that you have established; what are human beings that you are mindful of them, mortals that you care for them? Yet...! Yet...!

Yet here we are immersed and drenched in what Dillard calls the "Scandal of particularity." God has noticed you and me. God has singled us out. God loves us and has a plan for our life is how the evangelicals put it. It is our Father's good pleasure to give us the kingdom is how the Bible puts it. But the sad fact is that most of us don't know what to do with the kingdom that is given. Many of us don't even seem to know there is a kingdom. We continue to live fearfully, striving for all the wrong motives for all the wrong treasures, treasures that won't last, treasures that can't resist the onslaught of rust and moths, treasures that don't even belong to the kingdom we are being given.

Jesus taught us to consider the birds and the lilies. They both do what they were made to do. They do what they must do according to their nature. Birds fly, lilies bloom. They eat what is given and grow by nutrition which is also given. They are un-self-conscious. God knows what they need; God created them and determined their need in advance. And God appointed in advance that the rest of creation would supply their need, according to God's riches in glory.

Jesus assures us that God has not done less than this for us, but even more. As Paul wrote, "My God will supply all your need according to His riches in glory." If the extravagant display before us every day in the creation that is nothing short of promiscuous in its scope and variety and is so massive and deep that even the most keen observer among us ends up mute in awe and wonder, what are we to make of such a station as ours described in Psalm 8 as being a little lower than the angels and sharing dominion of such a magnificent world? God promises to meet our needs, but the real gift is that God invests our lives with divine purpose. We are to do more than work to eat and eat to work. In addition to eating and working, we have been appointed to reign with Christ over the creation when it is redeemed and glorified and delivered from its bondage to decay and death.

A Fellowship of Cracked Pots

I am easily annoyed by advertising. I am like a detective on alert for the clues and cues that someone is trying to manipulate me. Maybe I'm just paranoid. I love the old saying that says, "Just because you're paranoid doesn't mean they're not out to get you." When it comes to the culture of consumerism I've developed a thin skin and a quick temper. I talk to, sometimes yell at, the people on TV: Shut up you liar; etc, etc.

One ad that annoys me has a kindly, grey bearded sage walking along a line of large rectangles forming a bar chart, with smiling, smart people following in his wake. He is urging me to have a planned saving strategy that over time will yield a secure retirement, "so you can live the life you've always dreamed of." And, oh, by the way, if you invest with us, well, you're almost home free. Trust my company to get you there.

Look, I know the magic of compound interest, I know the wisdom of financial planning, I know it's right to not be in the habit of letting your expenses exceed your income (a fact that our politicians routinely ignore); I know all that and don't disagree with any of it, except the dream at the end part. Along the way to this retirement dreamland, there is nothing said in the ad about selling your possessions and giving alms, and there is no warning that all this wealth can be quickly snatched away by a man in a three-pieced suit carrying a briefcase and driving a Porsche.

Jesus says that we should make purses for ourselves that do not wear out, and unfailing treasure in heaven, where no thief comes near and no moth destroys. How do you make such a purse for yourself?

You get the first bit of instruction a few verses prior to our text this morning where Jesus says, "Do not worry about your life." V.22. Don't worry about my life? What is Jesus, some kind of starry eyed idealist? No, Jesus simply understands that worry, anxiety, and fear will send you off on the wrong track, striving for things that God promises to provide.

Purse making in God's kingdom is a trust walk. I remember doing trust walks in youth group settings. One youth would be blindfolded and would have to trust the other members to lead him or her on a walk deprived of the ability to see. They had to trust their fellow youth not slam their nose into a wall or let them tumble down the church stairs. Another variation was to invite a kid to fall backwards, trusting the group members to catch them.

What God seems to want from us is generosity and what God also seems to want for us is freedom from worry. Both demand trust in the goodness and faithfulness of God. God teaches that the way into freedom is first to let go of what we think we have, what we think secures us, and to find our provision and security in working for God and the Kingdom.

Some of us are capable of constructing a small life wherein our ego feels secure and in control. The problem with such a life is that it is not expansive enough for the human spirit to become what God intended us to become. We end up investing in things too small. Our hearts shrivel down to size. Our lives become susceptible to the corrosive effects of living in the fallen world. We were created for much more than this.

I haven't been very skilled at preparing for retirement. I've been investing instead in the lives of people who will most likely never pay me back in money or any material things whatsoever. I've invested in the lives of my children and now in my grandchildren, and over the years in friends who found themselves in need. Lots of time, energy, commitment, service, and money have gone out.

That purse will not wear out because they are baptized people who are destined to live forever. Sometimes I think they waste what I give them. Sometimes I think they are foolish with my gifts. Sometimes I feel presumed upon. Sometimes I feel I'm being taken for granted. Sometimes I wonder if it's all just me serving to enable bad habits and fund sinful choices. Sometimes I wonder if I should have bought into the program offered by the kindly, grey-bearded man in the ad with his little dream of self-sufficiency.

Then I read the Bible.

Then the Holy Spirit helps me refocus and identify my treasure by saying, "Where is your heart Bill?" And the answer I know to be true for me is, "My treasure is in my faith and in my relationships. It is in my friendship with God. It is with my wife, and my children, and my grandchildren, and my life-long friendships, and with my fellow believers in the Body of Christ." I am truly a wealthy man, not because I am industrious, or clever, or disciplined in saving earthly treasures.

My true wealth is grounded in my love for God and my love for the people God has put in my life. Think of how much wealth we all have squandered by insisting on our own way with people. Remember Paul's counsel that we should count others better than ourselves, that we should have the same mind in us as is in Christ Jesus, a mind that consistently and persistently leads us to give ourselves away to each other, to outdo one another in showing honor?

None of these opportunities are mysterious so as to be beyond our ability to know what to do. We are each one of us afloat on a vast sea of opportunity to love other people generously and sacrificially. We all ought to have grown up by now to be master purse makers, purses that will be filled with the unfailing treasure of having pleased God. We please God very simply by loving the Lord our God with all our heart, soul, mind, and strength and loving our neighbor as ourselves. Jesus taught us that the simplest way to find and please God is to look for God in the faces, the lives, and the needs of the least of us. I remember Mother Teresa saying to someone who asked her why she wasted her time among the destitute and dying that she did it because it was in their faces that she most clearly saw the face of Christ. This is the whole Law and the core counsel of all the prophets. Everything else will pass away and leave us empty handed in the end.

If you want to craft a fine purse and fill it with lasting treasure, go find someone who needs love and love them. Go find someone who is hungry and feed them. Go find someone who is discouraged and encourage them. Go make a real investment in your real future and stop wasting time producing food for moths and metal for rust to devour.

Help for Hoarders

Our neighbor went through a painful, messy divorce (aren't most divorces painful and messy?). As part of the settlement she sold her home for just under ½ a million dollars and moved away. The next thing we knew, workmen's trucks began to show up, not just for days but for many months. The house was gutted, remodeled, expanded, and who knows what else. Tree surgeons and landscapers and all sorts of workers came and went. At last a young couple moved in with their young son and a newborn daughter. Workers continued to come and go. At Christmas, professional decorators arrayed the house and trees with many strings of white lights.

I met the young man once when I was out for a walk and saw him at the mailbox. I introduced myself and welcomed him to the neighborhood. The only other time I had any interaction with him was when I asked him to help me blow out my driveway entrance during last winter's wet snow. I never met his wife. I met their nanny a few times. I only saw their son a couple of times. Workers continued to come and go.

The week before last, landscapers mulched extensively. The tree company came and cut down some trees and trimmed some others. Then much to our surprise, a huge moving van showed up this week and packed them up.

Jean and I kept looking out the window, wondering what in the world was going on. Were they alright? Was there a divorce? Was there some problem with the house that money couldn't solve? Was it after all just too small for their taste and level achieved in life? What? Finally, I joked with Jean that we were acting like two nosey old people like you might see on a TV show like Keeping Up

Appearances, peeking into other people's business instead of minding our own. But still, I wonder. After all that, where have they gone and why? And how did they so quickly accumulate enough stuff to fill a large moving van and still leave behind three of those bagsters full of trash?

Human hoarding has a long history predating our very American propensity to consume things and pile up the leftovers in our attics, basements, and garages. It must have been a stumbling block even in Jesus' day. Jesus told a parable about it in Luke 12.

The parable he told was a parable about a rich man who was a greedy fool. What preceded the parable came through a man in the crowd following Jesus who wanted Jesus to mediate a family fight over an inheritance. It seems that most families sooner or later get around to fighting over someone's will. Someone grabs an unfair share and someone else becomes jealous and bitter over the injustice done.

But Jesus could spot an emotional triangle a mile off. In case you don't know what that is, an emotional triangle arises when two people in conflict or under stress seek a third party to dump their excess psychic load upon. We learn this as early as childhood: "Mom, he took my toy. Make him give it back!" Teens are already master triangle builders: "Dad, can I stay out all night and take the car to Atlantic City. Mom said it was alright with her if it is alright with you." Adults do it too: "Pastor, I can't make my husband come to church. Every time I bring it up, he tells me to quit nagging him. Maybe you could talk to him."

We also use triangles to escape expectations of others: "I'd love to honey, but my boss expects me at work," or, "My golfing buddies are expecting me; I don't want to let them down." There are nine million variations of emotional triangles that people use on each other to escape personal responsibility in relationships. Do you get it? When things get hot and heavy, we go looking for someone else to bear our relational difficulties for us.

"Jesus, tell my brother to be fair and do what's right." Jesus swiftly and deftly avoided being triangled in to this man's scheme. Jesus immediately reached below the surface of the aggrieved man's request and issued him a warning: "Take care! Be on your guard against all kinds of greed; for one's life does not consist in the abundance of possessions." Evidently the man's cry for justice was nothing more than a clever mask for his greed. And Jesus knew that greed was a dead-end street. Jesus knew that the common wisdom of that day was that personal wealth was a sign to the rest of the community that a person was blessed by God and was a moral cut above everyone else. And some thought that greed would take them to the top and they would receive public acclaim as one righteous before God. "He must be holy; look how God has blessed him."

So, Jesus told a parable with a punch line that exposed a greedy rich man as a fool in the end. What made him a fool? The rich man had a banner year, so much so that he didn't have enough room to hoard his goods. His answer was to make more room. There is nothing wrong with wealth. And the trouble was not even his new barn building project, unless you want to condemn him for not turning toward his less fortunate neighbors and giving his stuff away. [Sometimes reading the Bible is like reading today's paper, especially during political campaigns.] Social justice may in fact require acts of generosity from the rich to the poor. We don't call it generosity; we call it reforming the tax code. But even this wasn't the real danger being faced by the man in the story.

The real problem was not with the man's wealth, it was the conclusion he drew from his unexpected blessings. He said to his soul, "Soul, you have ample goods laid up for many years; relax, eat, drink, and be merry." He was saying that the highest aspiration in his life was comfort, ease, entertainment, and the satisfaction of his appetites. The testimony of people, who take early retirement with the agenda to fill up their lives with hobbies and other recreational activities they've put on hold while working, is that they find themselves going crazy after about six months. It seems that the human soul needs to retain a higher aspiration than amusing ourselves to death.

Jesus parable concludes with God saying to the rich man, "You fool! This very night your life is being demanded of you. And the things you have prepared, whose will they be? So, it is with those who store up treasures for themselves but are not rich toward God."

The Apostle Paul picks up on the rich man's message to his soul in his discussion of the resurrection in I Corinthians 15. There he says that if Christ has not been raised, "Eat, drink, and be merry, for tomorrow we die." Here there is help for hoarders of all stripes. I'll return to this in a minute, but first things first.

Many of us have a history of struggling with hoarding things. We do it for a variety of reasons. For some it is greed. Greed piles up things for the comfort of having piles of things. The abundance offers its own reward, paltry though it is in the long run. People ought to rise higher than a pack rat's delight in things that merely glitter and shine, but sadly, some get caught right there. Treasure that is susceptible to moth and rust will disappoint us and vanish in the end. It gives the illusion of being real wealth but it isn't.

For some like my father who grew up during the Great Depression, hoarding begins as an attempt to be a steward, to not waste things that still have potential usefulness, if not to us, to some unspecified someone. The problem with unspecified "someones" is that they often never show up to claim the prize you've been saving just for them. Or if they do show up, they don't want what you have to offer.

Then there is a third category of hoarders. I suspect for many, if not for most, hoarding is a mask for fear. We have fear and anxiety about tomorrow, even though Jesus tells us, and Paul does too: "Have no anxiety about anything." The antidote to our anxious fears is faith in the goodness and intensive care taken by God on our behalf.

As soon as we leave the door to anxiety open, even if just a small crack, the battle is on. "Will I have enough? Will I have what I need? What will happen if I don't store this or that somewhere? As sure as you're born, the day I throw it away, the next day I'll wish I hadn't." As my dad said every time he stashed a little treasure away, "I might need this someday." He's been gone thirty years, and I still have some of the things he might have needed but never did. Now as I try to simplify my own life, I have the burden of disposing of many things that I never even knew why he saved them.

Storing up treasures for myself and yourself doesn't just take up space; it uses up energy, intelligence, imagination, and even love. It can lead us into a place of greed, which always seems to thrive at someone else's expense. Families fight over things. "Teacher, tell by brother to divide the family inheritance with me." Relationships are devoured that once were characterized by mutual love and respect. The cure? Become rich toward God.

Become rich toward God because God is already rich toward you. God knows what you need. God knows how to bless you. God knows how to keep you. God causes his face to shine upon you.

God knows how to replace your anxious fears with the peace that passes understanding. If we spent even a fraction of our lives seeking to be rich in God we would see the tide turning in this life.

I came across an aphorism by Annie Dillard the other day that struck me. She wrote, "The way we spend our days is the way we are spending our lives." I wrote it in my journal. "The way we spend our days is the way we are spending our lives." How are you spending your days? Your life is speeding by at a one day at a time rate. That sentence is a reminder to me that my life is not the grand sweep of decade after decade. Today is really the only day I have.

My past is gone; it is either still filled with guilt, shame and the memory of past wounds, or it is the storehouse of God's grace. My future is not yet. Its storehouse may be filled with fear, anxiety, and worry. Or its storehouses may be filled with confidence in God, with faith, hope, and trust in God's commitment to my wellbeing in all times.

My present life is, and so is yours, a daily investment in something or other. I'll say it again: The present is the only time I have. It's the only time you have. And it is in the daily-ness of our living where we are either becoming fools or becoming rich toward God. And the choices we make are used somehow in the overall outcome, in the assessment of how we have done with our one and only, precious life, the life bought with the precious blood of Jesus Christ, the risen Son of the Living God.

God has made the first choice. God has chosen you. Is it too much for God to ask that we choose God in return? God makes us first; we are to make God first. The alternative is to be judged as a fool when our life is demanded.

Jesus Behind Closed Doors

Today would have been our son Jonathan's 35th birthday. Later on today I will do what I have been doing since he moved on to be with the Lord. I will write him a letter in my journal, which of course is not really for him but for me. The practice keeps me in touch with an important place in my heart that I don't want to forget or bury. It's a place where love is still alive for the son I can no longer speak with or touch or do much of anything with except remember. Losing him the way we did makes me all the more thankful for the grace of God. I have with confidence commended him to God's mercy. I know he is safe home.

One year ago on this date, on Jon's birthday, Mark and I set out for Santiago from St. Jean in southern France, walking the 500 mile Camino together. One of the favorite tidbits of Camino wisdom is that the first third is about the body, the second third is about the soul, and the last third is about the spirit. It ended up being true for the most part.

The spiritual life is like that in many respects. We go through stages of development as we walk with Christ. And the longer we walk the more dominant the reality of grace becomes. Sooner or later if we keep going long enough we come to realize that our faith is grace from top to bottom, from start to finish; it is grace through and through. God's grace is relentless and will not let us get off track for very long before it seeks us out in our waywardness and puts our feet back on the right path.

One day on the Camino, I met a delightful man, a Roman Catholic layperson who said his mission in life was waking up dead Catholics. I got a hearty chuckle out of that, since sometimes I've thought of my ministry as helping to thaw the frozen chosen. We met repeatedly along the path. Near the end he told me of a day when some people had attached themselves to him and were walking alongside for some time. Somewhere, Michael lost touch with the yellow way markers that guide pilgrims along the Camino. He hadn't seen a yellow arrow in quite a while. When he announced that they were off the track and he was doubling back, his new companions began to argue with him. They didn't want to admit their error. To retrace their steps seemed like too much work. He said, "You do what you want. I'm going back." It was the right correction to make.

Thomas the disciple was like that. He was one of the original twelve. He'd been walking with Jesus for three years. He had about as much faith as was needed as long as Jesus was alive and leading the way. He had no reason to doubt and many experiences to confirm that this was a man worth following. He saw the miracles, signs, and wonders. He was there when Jesus fed a huge crowd with only a boy's small lunch. He was in the boat when Jesus calmed the storm. He'd witnessed firsthand the healings, the mighty acts of deliverance, and even the raising of the dead. He had stood in awe as Jesus took on the head theologians and religious professors and bested them in power and wisdom every time. In short, he had plenty of evidence to make a believer out of him.

Then calamity had struck and his belief just seemed to evaporate right before his eyes. Mighty death seemed to have undone all of his confidence. He felt like a fool. He felt like he'd been duped. And he made a vow with himself never to let it happen again. He recited my dad's favorite motto: "Fool me once, shame on you; fool me twice, shame on me." Thomas had come a long way, but now he had veered off course. He needed a course correction.

Maybe you too have had this experience. You were sailing along just fine, your faith seeming to be in full bloom like a spring flower. Then calamity struck. The diagnosis came and it was not good, the child died, the husband left, or you were betrayed or abandoned or taken advantage of by someone you trusted. The life you envisioned and the dreams you dreamed went up in smoke. You felt like a fool. You began to lose your belief and slide over into unbelief. It happened to Thomas. It can happen to you and me. Thank God that's not the end of the story. It's more like the prelude to a new and deeper beginning. Course corrections are the norm in the disciple's life.

The footnotes to my study Bible have it correct. This story is not so much about Thomas's doubt. It is really a story about the grace of Jesus. In fact, the main issue for Thomas is not doubt, which is only a function of the mind which demands reasons to be given for everything. No, his real issue according to the scripture is unbelief, which is a category involved with faith.

Faith is deeper than reason. Faith seeks understanding, but faith is a gift from God which makes the search possible. When Jesus tells Thomas, "Do not doubt, but believe," he is challenging Thomas to go deeper. We have mistakenly and habitually spoken of doubting Thomas. We say to one another, "Don't be a doubting Thomas." But as I said, doubt wasn't his main problem. His main problem was unbelief, which is deeper than doubt and much harder to root out of his soul and of our souls as well. The opposite of belief is not doubt, it is unbelief. Jesus wants faith which is an expression of the belief made possible by the ministry of the Holy Spirit convincing the human heart that we are beloved of God and that Jesus is Lord and God.

The question is, how do we cross over the chasm that separates unbelief from belief. And what do we need when life's circumstances hurl us backward from belief to unbelief? Notice that the demands of Thomas were essentially the same as those of the other ten disciples on the first Easter. He too demanded to see the wounds of Jesus just as they said they had seen them. In spite of all he had witnessed with Jesus during his ministry, he still needed a deeper convincing. His eyes demanded to see. His mind would not change unless his eyes could see and his hands could touch. Many if not most people are likewise bound by what they can see and what they feel. But sight and feeling don't go deep enough to sustain any of us.

When Mary announced that Jesus was alive and had appeared to her the ten were unwilling to believe her. They treated her like a hysterical woman when she showed up to tell them she had seen the risen Christ. Then and there, behind closed and locked doors, the doors of fear and unbelief, Jesus had shown up. Then and there, behind closed doors, he showed them his wounds. There was mighty power in these marks that from a worldly point of view were the evidence of Jesus' weakness, not his strength. But God's weakness is stronger than the strength of human brutality and violence, of our suspicions and fears and hatreds. Jesus pronounced peace upon them at the moment when they might have expected retribution for this wounding at human hands.

And Jesus spoke of sending them to continue his mission and his work in the world, which centered upon forgiveness. He was teaching them that the godly response to wounding is not revenge but forgiveness. He entrusted to them the message of reconciliation between humanity and God and between one human and another. The inherent enmity which characterized fallen humanity before Good Friday had been overcome through the Cross and Resurrection. Now it was time for all faith filled disciples to live life in light of that fact.

Along the Camino as Michael and I shared our life stories while we walked the ancient pilgrim way, he told me a very powerful tale. His grandmother had been viciously murdered and the murderer had been arrested and brought to trial. His whole family was swept up in a vortex of anger, bitterness, and unforgiveness. They sought the vengeance that justice would bring. The murderer was convicted but the rage continued on within his family. The conviction did not bring comfort or release.

Then one night, Michael had a powerful dream in which the Virgin Mary appeared to him and told him that he must go and speak to Mother Teresa who had a scheduled visit to LA where he lives. He woke up suddenly. The dream was powerful and Mary seemed so real. But how does one insignificant man get to see such a sought after and world famous figure like Mother Teresa? It's one thing to have a powerful dream. It's another to arrange a significant encounter with a very famous person when one is awake.

A short time later as he walked through the evening darkness down a small side street in LA a door suddenly opened and two ladies emerged who were bidding goodbye to another woman in the doorway. The woman was Mother Teresa. She pointed to him and beckoned him to come in. As they sat in two simple chairs opposite one another, Michael proceeded to tell the story of his troubled soul and of his embittered family. Then, convicted in the presence of this slight and humble sister he said, "I know. I guess I'm going to have to forgive him." And Mother Teresa reached across and laid her hand on his thigh and said, "Not enough to forgive! You must love!" He was struck as though by lightening by the power of the Holy Spirit. Through that encounter, Michael was able to let go and brought healing to his whole family. Forgiveness is the most powerful source of healing there is.

In the graciousness of the Lord Jesus, he gave Thomas what he needed to believe. He invited him to not only see, but to reach out and touch his wounds. The wounds of Christ carry with them the power to heal us. He uses them as an emblem of forgiveness. They carry within them the power to convince us of the depth of the love of God for us. The wounds were the thing that finally caused the ten disciples who first saw them to break forth with rejoicing. The joy that comes with encountering the risen Christ burst from them like a mighty rushing river of living water. And for Thomas, it was the sight of those same wounds and the invitation to touch them that caused his confession to come forth with the astonishment they deserve: "My Lord and my God!" Christ's wounds authenticate his completed work.

Jesus' words: "Have you believed because you have seen me? Blessed are those who have not seen and yet have come to believe." With those words, the Gospel was set loose upon the world. If you are already a believer, did you hear? You who have not yet seen [someday you will] and yet believe are called blessed. And if you don't believe, what stands in your way? Usually it is something as insignificant as intellectual pride which thinks doubting is a mark of sophistication. It is not. It is simply the mark of human stubbornness which refuses to be loved by God. Doubt is not much more than a waste of time and a waste of life. The insistence of doubt signals that one is still living in a closed universe that has no place for mystery, for awe, and for wonder. The doubter lives in a small, flattened world where there are no miracles or signs that point to the transcendent nature of reality.

John ends this chapter with these words: "Now Jesus did many other signs in the presence of his disciples, which are not written in this book. But these are written so that you may come to believe that Jesus is the Messiah, the Son of God, and that through believing you may have life in his name."

Lord I believe. Remove from me all unbelief, all doubt, all fear of being tricked, all pride that thinks that faith in you is nothing more than intellectual credulity. Give me enough courage to become a believer in Jesus Christ and to receive the life promised through his name.

Keep on Keeping On

The sermon began with impromptu interviews with worshippers...

Okay, let's debrief what just happened. When I first took to the aisle, some of you were thinking, "Oh no; now what's he up to?" As I approached you, you were a little uneasy. I invaded your personal space. You were hoping my intention was not to embarrass you. You'll notice that I was trying to be respectful (I hope). I had no agenda to recruit you for some kind of church work like serving as a greeter, an usher, or to teach a Sunday school class. My interviews were simply conversations. We shared a moment of life together in an intimate interaction among the others worshipping here today.

You may have been surprised. You may have enjoyed it. You may have thought it was totally inappropriate, that you didn't come here for such an activity. You may cherish your privacy, your individual space which is not to be invaded by some crazy preacher, or your anonymity. To you in that group, I offer my most insincere apology! You see, I have a pastoral purpose for what I've just done.

I want to explore a topic dear to my heart, the topic of prayer. I've tried for my whole Christian life to become a man of prayer. It was in prayer that I first discovered that God was not just an idea, not just some imagined, white-bearded heavenly grandfather figure, and certainly was not someone to be lied to or manipulated.

As a young man, I became deeply mired in my own sinfulness. My appetites were leading me around as though by a ring in my nose. When my good friend Joe died right before my eyes, I didn't know what else to do but try to pray. And to my shock, I was answered by the God who is real. And God's answer to all of my attempts to pray was very terse: "You're lying!" After several attempts to dress up my speech with no success, the Lord said very clearly in my soul, "The reason you cannot pray without lying is because the truth is not in you. If you don't give your life to me, you will live your life walking around as dead as Joe is."

I gave my heart to God on an "if you're out there" basis with the request, "Please just make it real. I don't want to waste any more time on what is not true."

Several months later, I was reading the Gospel of John and got to know Jesus personally. "How?" you might ask, to which I will say one word, "Grace." The God who was for me "out there" became the God who is in here, inside my heart by the Holy Spirit. So, I began my Christian life with the knowledge that conversation with God was available to me personally and I began my journey of developing my communication skills with God. In one word, we call those skills prayer. But when we speak of prayer in the same breath with the word skills, we should be careful.

Communication is multilayered, whether in ordinary conversation with a person or in prayer with God. It involves not just talking but listening. And listening skills are multifaceted. I've taught whole courses on what is called active listening. Active listening goes beyond hearing the surface words. You must learn to read things like body language and to discern meanings that lie beneath the surface. You must learn to use language that opens up deeper levels of truth and vulnerability rather that shutting communication down with what are known as verbal villains. You must learn how to keep the focus upon the speaker who is sharing and not divert the conversation so that everything is all about you, or your uncle, or your great-grandfather who had the same problem 100 years ago. And so on and on it goes.

I say all this not in order to teach you about active listening this morning. I'm attempting to crack the door open into our passage from Luke 11. The disciples had been walking around with Jesus for some time, listening to him teach, and watching him work. They saw miracles, signs, and wonders. People were healed. A few were even brought back from the dead, alive as ever. Jesus won every argument with people in power, whether political or religious. Throngs of hungry people were fed, lepers were cleansed, and demons were expelled.

Everywhere Jesus went, lives were changed. It was amazing! And they saw Jesus praying, or they saw him leave them behind for a while to go pray alone. He prayed sometimes before miracles. He prayed for miracles which then happened. He prayed after miracles. He prayed when he was sad, when he was tired, and when he was thankful. He prayed in danger. He prayed all the time.

It must have finally dawned on the disciples that there had to be a connection with the quality of life Jesus lived, the things he was able to do, and prayer. And finally, they wanted in on it. So, they came to Jesus and said, "Lord, teach us to pray. John the Baptist taught his disciples to pray. Why don't you do as much for us?"

Jesus didn't hesitate, even to take a breath. He could have questioned them: "Why do you want to know? What do you hope to gain? What do you think prayer is?" Etc. etc. But he cut right to the chase: "When you pray say this…" He gave them what we call the Lord's Prayer, which is really the prayer that the Lord gave to the disciples. It is short and sweet and every word and phrase is simple and packed with life. I could preach a whole series of sermons on that brief prayer; in fact, I have done so in the past. Let's just say the prayer's petitions map out our very personal and intimate relations with God and with each other.

A Fellowship of Cracked Pots

Let me emphasize the two words personal and intimate as I press on to the latter half of our passage, the part that is too often treated as separate from the Lord's Prayer. I want to suggest it is intimately tied to it. It's the part that says, picking up the sense of the Greek texts which does not come through in English translation: ask and keep on asking, seek and keep on seeking, knock and keep on knocking, and you will receive and find and discover the door through which you seek entrance will swing wide open to you.

I've read a hundred books, maybe more, on prayer. This is how you do it; that is how you do it. Say this, believe that, do it this way, do it that way, or combine it with this discipline, or do it this often, or sit or walk or stand on your head; it seems there is no end to techniques of praying that guarantee success. I've tried most just to see what would happen. I've heard about the studies that "prove" that patients prayed for recover at a greater rate than those not prayed for. If you've been sick, we've prayed for you. I've heard televangelists take credit for everything from healing people to diverting the path of hurricanes and stopping the advance of forest fires.

I've heard that I must picture outcomes in my mind and that I must try real hard to exercise my faith. I've heard that I must take authority, learn how to rebuke this or that evil, or that I must step out into this or that endeavor as though the result has already come, I just couldn't see it; this is described as faith.

There may be, probably are, kernels of truth in almost all of this teaching and in all of these testimonies, but let me simply say that I have come to a different place, a place that I would say is personal and intimate.

When I walked among you a few minutes ago, for me it was personal and intimate. I wasn't practicing my active listening skills.

I wasn't trying some technique on you to try to get something from you. I was simply showing loving interest in your life. I was merely building a tiny bridge between your heart and mine. The flow of love and interest and respect was its own reward.

I think Jesus was anticipating the question that often arises in prayer which is, "What if I pray and nothing happens? What if I pray and I don't get an answer? What if I knock on the door and God is in bed, or too busy, or preoccupied with more important things; then what?"

It's almost as though Jesus is waving a caution sign at us. Prayer may not be what you think. It may not be a way to get the attention of God who already sees and knows everything. It may not be a magical tool to stimulate an uncaring deity to "do something."

My late mentor Dr. Loder told a story of being a young man who was called home from college because his beloved father was sick unto death. He shared his experience of finally coming to a fit of rage before the Lord and screaming out, "Do something! For God's sake, why don't you do something?" Instantly a shock like a strong bolt of electricity shot through his entire body as he lay on the bed in his room. That experience changed the quality of his relationship with God for ever.

Could it be that there is something important for us to discover encased in those experiences which demand perseverance. There have been times between Jean and me where she was trying hard to get something through my thick husband skull, trying with no visible signs of success. If the issue was important to her, she just kept trying. And because she is supremely important to me, I kept trying to understand as well. We have tended to get there eventually, together. We'll celebrate 45 years married this November.

But what I want you to know is that the intimacy achieved after the period of struggle has almost always been worth it. It has been deeper and more substantial. She could have given up. I could have gone into my man-cave saying, "I don't care; have it your way honey." And what she'd have heard is, "I don't care." The outcome of giving up would have been bitterness and disappointment. And the next time around, expectations would have been lower until one or both of us just stopped trying. People give up on one another, all too often. And all too often, people give up on God because they fail to understand what Jesus was teaching about persevering in asking, searching, and knocking on the door of the heart of God.

Perhaps the point of the perseverance seasons of prayer is that we will eventually discover just how much God does care. God cares so deeply that God himself will enter our darkest hours, and "even though I walk through the valley of the shadow of death, I will fear no evil," to quote Psalm 23. Perhaps after a season of perseverance we'll have a much deeper insight into the love God has for us, a love that caused his beloved Son to forsake all of his heavenly estate, empty himself, and humble himself, even unto death on the cross devised by the sinners he came to save. His crime was love, and for that he died among us. And by that same love, he rose again from the dead and led captivity captive, parading the enemies of God's goodness through the streets of eternity as defeated foes.

Jesus granted the disciples request to be taught to pray with a very simple but powerful prayer, and then in so many words said, "It's not so much how you do it, it's that you do it, and keep on doing it, no matter what. Enter into the conversation that is prayer; enter into the intimacy that grows as you keep at it over the long haul. You will develop a deeply personal relationship with us, with Father, Son, and Holy Spirit which will open to you a quality of life that is always given, never earned and never manipulated from the heart of God by your silly techniques.

More Than We Can Bear No More

"I have many things to say to you but you cannot bear them now."

What unwelcome words! I'm sure they've been said to you a time or ten in your life, usually, though not always, in a situation of conflict or disagreement. When we get irritated or frustrated with the dim bulb standing before us, we reach the point where we begin to say things like, "You just don't understand," or "You'll never get it!", or "There's no way I can explain this to you that you'll be able to comprehend it," or "When you get to be my age," or "It's just because you are old and set in your ways," or "Someday, when you're older, wiser, smarter, more caring, more loving, more humble"....and so on, and so and on and on. Most of the time, when someone points out our limitations, we get defensive. It's a put down. We don't appreciate being judged to be inadequate or incomplete. We get offended, insulted, or even angry.

The disciples had left everything to follow Jesus. They'd been on what amounted to a three-year camping trip. Foxes had holes, and birds of the air had nests, but the Son of Man had nowhere to lay his head. "Where are you staying Lord?" "Come and see," Jesus answered. They ended up staying wherever they ended up after long days of walking, and listening, and learning.

The disciples had dutifully submitted to the rigors of following Jesus, and they'd seen and even done remarkable things. How could Jesus say, "There is so much more, but you're not ready." They must have thought, "If we're not ready yet, we'll never be. How much more preparation could there be? We've demonstrated that we're all in for Jesus. Bring on the Kingdom! Pour out the promised blessings! Make us happy and fulfilled."

The problem for them is still the problem for us. Jesus seems to have something beyond happiness and personal fulfillment in store, not just for us but for the whole world. And the things he had yet to say to the disciples had to wait until a fundamental change took place in their deepest heart. It's the same for you and me.

Transformation seems on the surface to be a desirable thing. We hear the word and envision a smooth process of going from good to better to best. We tend to see it as the result of a gradual learning curve as our lives ripen like fruit on the vine, the flavor of our lives becoming ever richer with complex overtones and undertones like a fine, vintage wine. The problem with this view is that it omits a key ingredient of transformation which is the crisis component. You must be born again, and for the new to be born, the old must die. Death to self is always a crisis to self.

Many of us are like Nicodemus. We don't get it at first. Disciples, then and now, start off not being able to comprehend the connection between dying and rising. But there can be no rising from death if there is not first a death from which to rise. At this point in John's Gospel, the disciples had not yet experienced Holy Week. Jesus warned them about the cross. They said, "May it never be! This shall not happen to you Lord, not as long as we can help it!" Jesus told them they were thinking and speaking like the devil: "Get behind me Satan; you are not on God's side but men's!"

Peter and the rest of the disciples had yet to go through the strainer of Good Friday, of seeing their master captured, humiliated, tortured, and nailed up for all to see. They had yet to descend into the tunnel of fear and despair of that dark, silent Saturday when Jesus lay in the dark and sealed tomb as all their hopes were dashed and their dreams of being in the inner circle of the Kingdom of God were visibly crushed by Roman imperial might. They had no Easter yet, with its empty tomb. They were still on the far side of the resurrection. They lived in the world where dead men don't rise, ever (except for a few notable anomalies like Lazarus and the dead son of the widow from Nain). The astonished amazement of Jesus alive again yet lay in an invisible future.

They had a world view that had stood the test of time. When you die, you're dead. Maybe you do go on in some other dimension, maybe you don't. The scribes and the Pharisees each had their own opinions, just like people today have lots of opinions about what happens after we die. The world created by the expectations of our human egos must first to be shattered before we ever become able to fathom the expansive vision that God has for making the whole world new. And in like manner, they had no way to conceive of the part God would expect them to play in the ongoing work of redeeming the world from sin and even death. For the most part, neither do we.

The worlds we create for ourselves are realms which our egos will tenaciously defend. Transformation is no friend of ego centricity. The ego has neither desire nor intention of being dragged to Golgotha and there be crucified. We carefully cultivate our hopes for life, liberty, and the pursuit of happiness. This is the basic mantra of our beloved nation. Our ideals are noble but they lose much of their nobility when they become only a narcissistic concern for "my life, my liberty, and my happiness." Jesus calls us to a deeper concern and a transformed awareness.

In the Kingdom of God, the quality of my life is tied directly to the quality of yours. If you are diminished, so am I. The ego centric "me" is not yet ready to hear that. It's a word that my flesh can't bear. It makes no sense and can even be perceived as a threat. Further, is my liberty full as long as your liberty has been stomped by oppression? Is my happiness true happiness if it is purchased at your expense?

You might use these questions as a tool for discernment during our season of political debate leading to the presidential elections. Just beware! Politicians of all stripes are known for making promises they can't keep.

God never makes promises God can't keep. And God is wise enough to know what we are ready to hear and what we are not yet ready to hear. God's restraint and timing are acts of mercy, not insults to draw attention to our limitations. God alone knows how radical and difficult transformation can be for people like us. We can be so fearful, so obstinate, so un-teachable, and so self-defended.

When the call that comes demands dying to all that is too small in order to expand our capacity for those things that God deems great, we either dig in or run away. We must learn to breathe the air of humility, which for proud mammals like us is about as easy as learning to breathe under water.

When sociologists today study religion in America, they ask, "What religion are you? Or what is your religious preference?" The fastest growing demographic in our nation is the group that checks to box labeled "None." The "religious nones" is how they are labeled.

Sadly, I've witnessed the growth of this group among parents who bring their children to be baptized, and then disappear until the children are grown and the families want a church wedding. Then the couple stands before God, take their vows, and afterward disappear again until a new generation comes to be baptized, or until someone dies and they want a funeral service.

Okay, there is no condemnation for those who are in Christ. But still I am left to wonder, where do they hear the call to transformation out there in the world whose main agenda is life, liberty, and the pursuit of happiness. It is easy to shrink the world down to encompass mainly what concerns me and my immediate family. Am I living the quality of life to which I feel entitled? Am I free to do whatever I darn well please and to buy whatever I have enough money to afford? Am I happy, and if I'm not, what promises and commitments must I break and forsake so that nothing inconvenient stands between me and my right to be satisfied no matter what?

Jesus calls us to a larger vision. Who in the world sounds the call? Are we living in a time like the inter-testamental period between Malachi and the revelation we call the New Testament, where the prophets' voices have grown silent and people are left to somehow find their own way through the morass of confusion we call the modern world in which everyone simply does what is right in his or her own eyes?

Sadly, even the church loses her trumpet from time to time. In the name of the separation of church and state, have we too laid down our horns and become irrelevant in the world? The silence is deafening. And are people drifting away because irrelevance breeds apathy at best and outright resentment and hostility at worst?

Today is Trinity Sunday. In light of what has just been said, listen again to the words of Jesus in John 16: *"I still have many things to say to you, but you cannot bear them now. When the Spirit of truth comes, he will guide you into all the truth; for he will not speak on his own, but will speak whatever he hears, and he will declare to you the things that are to come. He will glorify me, because he will take what is mine and declare it to you. All that the Father has is mine. For this reason, I said that he will take what is mine and declare it to you."*

Do you think it is time for us finally to become ready, willing, and able to bear all that Jesus has to say to us? Do you think we might begin to fathom what he meant when he said that all the Father has is his and he is in the process of passing all of that on to us? It's an outrageous statement. What would happen to our world view and our life maps if we began to live in its light?

In the last few minutes, I have bombarded you with question after question. It is no way to preach a sermon usually. Usually, one or two questions are enough. I've been poking and prodding you in an attempt to send you out wondering: "Is my god too small; and are my parameters too constricted?"

In light of the magnificent interplay between Father, Son, and Holy Spirit, in light of the dynamism of the love that surges among those three persons of the godhead, and in light of Jesus' promise to catch each believer up into the whirlwind of the love of God and then send us out into his good creation as ambassadors of that redeeming, renewing, freshly creative love, have I yet truly discovered my real life, my true liberty, and my blessedness at God's hand that makes mere happiness seem but a shallow substitute for what God has done in Christ for me and what God intends to do by the Holy Spirit through me?

My guess is that the honest answer for each one of us must be, "No, not yet. I have so far been unable to bear such words and such promises. But now, I'm willing to listen and learn. Now my appetite for mere religion has been transformed into a deep hunger to know God and serve Jesus Christ as a transformed person."

I don't know about you. I can speak to you but I can't speak for you. I can only say that for me, my prayer is: "Lord, get to it! I am yours to do with as you see fit. I trust you to transform me, to bring me through whatever dying I must do so that I can get on with whatever living you want me to do, in Jesus' name. Amen."

Naked and Unafraid

3:28 AM, the wee hours of Thursday morning. Did you ever wonder what insomniac preachers think about as they lie awake in the dark, what goes thump in their night? Since I was lying awake anyway, I figured I'd think about my unwritten sermon on Hebrews 4. Then it struck: preacher fear. "Bill, you've totally lost touch with your congregation. What if they are not interested in spiritual transformation? What if they come to listen to sermons that would give them lots of information about the Bible that they would find merely interesting? What if they come to worship just to feel religious, to get a little up-lift as they say, and to garner a little support and encouragement for the life they have composed, all neat and under control, all cozy and predictable; then what?" I'd be over embellishing the story if I said I broke out in a cold sweat, but still.... In the bright light of Thursday morning I'm thinking, "Don't be silly. Of course, they want a sermon that cuts deep enough to change them from one degree of glory to the next. Why else would they give the time to listen to you? Give it another shot!" So, here we go. Are you ready?

In the sermon that is the Book of Hebrews, the preacher has been homing in on the majesty of Christ. He's been mining Israel's sacred history for his raw materials. The Jews believed that the Torah, the Law, had been delivered by angels to Moses. The preacher tells them that God had spoken in times past in all sorts of ways to all sorts of prophets, but in these last days God has spoken to us through His son. This son is far superior to angels in every way. There are angels who are God's messengers. Then there is the Son who is both messenger and the message rolled into one. So, pay attention Hebrews; something deeper is about to be revealed.

A Fellowship of Cracked Pots

Next the preacher shines his light on the priesthood whose ministry was so central to the religious life of Israel. Speaking of Moses and Aaron and the rest of the priesthood, the preacher argues that Jesus is far superior in his priesthood to those serving in the old covenant because he serves in God's house, not as a servant, but as a son. He is a servant, but also the rightful heir of all things. And Jesus is a high priest who is fully able to identify with us and represent us because he has shared in our humanity and suffered and been tempted in every way that we have. These are hallmarks of his servant hood. His superiority is not established by being unlike us and therefore high above us. It is established by his willingness to get right down in the mess we've made of the world and transform it from within. Jesus is the Son of God become one of us and one with us. The only difference between Jesus and us is that Jesus went through all that we do yet was without sin. He was totally faithful to his Father as a loving son. This means that neither we nor those Hebrews of so long ago have any need or warrant to be looking back or left or right, up or down, or in any other direction for a better representative to plead our case before God. Jesus is it. He is our perfect high priest.

As engrafted Gentile members of God's family, we may lose some of the force of these appeals to the Hebrews if we don't do a little work. When the preacher to the Hebrews summoned up material about the Exodus, about events in the wilderness, about Sabbath rest, and about angels and priests, the hearers were experiencing a direct touch on the raw nerves of their sacred traditions. These things ought not to be messed with; they are not open to transformation. They need to be preserved intact. The Presbyterian version of these objections is something like, "But we've never done it that way before."

But if we view this through the lens of spiritual transformation we know that people are constantly looking around, shopping for a better deal to see them through to the goal. Or worse, they are relying on old habits of religion trying to get back to the "good old days" and stay there. We like it the way it is; that's why it's the way it is.

Transformation tends to be radical. It brings deep changes that can seem overwhelming, even frightening. It involves leaving the known safety you have and launching into unknown territories which may or may not be safe. It's a long journey from Egypt to Canaan, from slavery to freedom, and from dull hopelessness to a life filled with promise. It is in the in-between space that trouble can show up. The old man does not give up without a fight. The wonder over manna soon dissolves into a yearning for the leeks, onions, and garlic, the stinky food of slavery. Resistance is always encountered on the path to transformation. You've met it every time you set out to go deeper with God. Every spiritual gain is contested. Count on it.

A pioneer of the therapeutic school known as family systems theory, Edwin Friedman, published a book titled, Friedman's Fables. In his fable titled, "The Bridge," he tells of a man who after many years had an opening to pursue a long-held dream. The opportunity would only be available for a short window of time. He decided to go for it and started on his way. Along the path he came to a bridge over a river gorge. About half way across the bridge, a man who looked much like himself approached from the other direction. He was carrying a large coil of rope with one end fastened around his waist. As they met, the man asked a favor. "Would you please hold the end of this rope for me?" The pilgrim agreed and took hold. At that, the man with the rope leapt over the rail of the bridge and plummeted about half way down to the bottom of the gorge where he hung suspended between life and death. He shouted up, "My life is in your hands now. Don't let go." Friedman details the unfolding of this drama in some detail. To

A Fellowship of Cracked Pots

condense it, finally the pilgrim realized that he did not have the strength to pull the man up, and that no help was coming. He began to plead with the man to pull himself up to safety. He refused, insisting that his life was in the pilgrim's hands. He held the power of life and death. It was his responsibility to save him. Sensing his long-desired opportunity was in danger of slipping away, his pity turned to anger. So, he gave the responsibility back to the dangling man: pull yourself up or I'm letting go. The choice is up to you." Our victim refused to climb and our pilgrim released his grip on the rope.

This fable is true on so many levels. It could be an illustration of someone whose dependence upon you has gone from real need to an irresponsible dependence. Sometimes victims of misfortune learn victimhood as a way of life and begin to live as users and abusers of those who have helped them. It could be so between a parent and a child, a husband and a wife, or between friends. When things get out of balance, pity quickly turns to anger. Something's got to give then. But I think the central point is that to reach our dreams we must let go. The pilgrim and the dangling man are one and the same person confronted by a choice.

Many people love the sound of words like freedom and promise, but when it comes to the process whereby we enter those things, we turn back in fear. Or we expect others to bear our spiritual responsibility to grow. Pray for me; your prayers are better than mine. Study for me and let me know what you've learned; I don't have time. Or we blame others: I would grow and change if it were not for her or him or that circumstance.

What's worse, people can get stuck in between bondage and freedom. They can end up dying spiritually in the land of complaint. That's what happened to those freed slaves of Egypt. Because entrance into Canaan inspired fear, they became grumblers and complainers. They became bitter toward Moses. Then they just plain got mad at God. They questioned God's goodness toward them. They yearned out loud for their old bondage. Finally, God had enough. "I swear you will never enter my rest," said God. "This generation will die in the wilderness." If you won't let go of your old life as slaves, you'll never know the peace open to those who enter a new life as sons and daughters. As Jesus rightly said to Nicodemus, "You must be born again or you will never see the kingdom of God."

Returning to Friedman's fable for one final turn, the dangling man, is the image of our old, ego controlled life, the one ticketed to be crucified with Christ so that our life that is raised with Christ may come to the fore. The fable is a picture of what happens on the cutting edge of transformation. A change of life is going on. The old life falls to its death. The new life crosses the bridge into the land of promise and opportunity.

Our dangling man or woman is deft at delaying the process. We learn with cleverness to mask our vanity as orthodoxy, our pride as piety, our flesh with religious forms and formalism, and put on fake smiles that run about as deep as one of those yellow smiley face stickers. The world is only part wrong when they say the church is nothing but a bunch of hypocrites, a collection of phony mask wearers. Churches do in fact harbor many who want the form of religion but deny its power.

But there are many, many like you perhaps, who come longing for something deeper, people who have a hunger to enter God's rest. To both groups the preacher to the Hebrews speaks. "Look out! The word of God is living and active, sharper than any two-edged sword. It has the capacity to separate things that don't belong together. The carefully crafted religious hiding places you've constructed will be sliced open. You will stand naked and afraid before God's judgment.

That is unless you put your faith in Christ. Then all will be different. The throne of judgment will be transformed for those who trust in Jesus Christ into the Throne of Grace. Before that throne, you need not fear. In the completed and ongoing priestly work of Christ, you have been given true peace and rest. In that provision, you are invited to approach with boldness. Bring your needs here. Here you will find mercy for all you have done. You've sinned and failed and made many mistakes; come boldly. Here both guilt and shame come to be silenced and to die. You have need of forgiveness. Come here! Come boldly! Mercy awaits.

You have needs for your current situation in life. Come boldly before the Throne of Grace. Grace is more than unmerited favor. It is the empowering gift of God that will enable you to become all that God intends for you. It is the open window of opportunity. It is the bridge across the chasms of defeat and despair that enables you to cross over into all the promises of God. It is the reality that takes shape after the old complaining, manipulative, mistrusting victim falls into death so that you can become one who knows how to live in the favor of God. Come boldly before the Throne of Grace. Tell of your need, your hunger, and your heart's true desire. You will receive help from the Throne of Grace. The throne is the emblem of rule, of sovereignty. God has seated Jesus there. He is your great high priest who totally understands you and who has the willingness and more than enough ability to help you. Come boldly!

Here's one final thing I want you to know. There is nothing better than transformation. And you are not in charge of the process. You participate, your choices and your cooperation are honored and dignified by God, but in the end, God is responsible to get you where you are going. And in Jesus Christ, God has shown you just how committed he is to success. God is committed enough to hang on the cross of our own devising. And God is powerful enough to negate the death administered there in the counter move called the resurrection. Life wins. Love wins. God is sovereign. God is good. Your good God and mine is the Lord of transformation and God wants you in on it, right now, and always.

Particle and Wave

I'm a liberal arts kind of man through and through. I'm not against science; I'm just no good at it. My awareness of scientific endeavors involves nothing but a mere smattering of things I've run across along my path of reading all the time. So, when I came across Jesus saying, "You are the light of the world," a little factoid floated up in my liberal arts brain. I remembered hearing somewhere that light was both particle and wave. I Googled it.

I randomly selected an article on the subject and began to read. It turns out that the scientific study of the nature of light goes back into the 1700s. I learned that some people thought light was a straight-line stream of photons while other people thought that light traveled in waves. As it turns out, both seem to be true at the same time. Light simultaneously behaves like particles and waves.

But how can that be. Our brains always want to resolve paradoxes toward one side or the other. We are most at home with either/or; both/and makes us uncomfortable. We'd rather sort than include. Think of all the wrestling in theology over Jesus, the God/man. "Which is he?" We want to know; is he human or divine? Our binary brains don't allow him to be both at the same time. But our faith and our theological reflection say that that's exactly what he is, the perfect union of humanity and divinity. It boggles the mind.

Getting back to my article on light, people wanted to know how fast light traveled. They wanted to find out if it slowed down when passing through something, like say, your car's windshield or a glass of water. They wanted to know how it behaved when reflected from a flat mirror. Particles were thought to bounce back at the same angle whereas waves would fan out erratically according to which part of the wave struck when. That's about as far as I got.

For the life of me I couldn't figure out how to work all this into my sermon on "You are the light of the world." My hair was beginning to hurt. I exited Google with a flick of my liberal arts index finger. I decided to stop trying to be so clever in ways I was not up to and just go to the text and see what would emerge. So here it is.

I'm sure you know that the very first Christians were all Jews who had grown up reading and studying and memorizing their Hebrew scriptures. When Jesus came along he opened their minds to understand those scriptures. He taught them how to see him promised and prophesied there. So they heard the words of Isaiah, for example, in a whole new way. "The people who walked in darkness have seen a great light. The people who dwelt in a land of deep darkness, on them has light shined." They began to hear and understand Bible verses in the light of Christ Jesus. It was a spiritual explosion in their souls.

John, the beloved disciple, began his gospel this way: "In the beginning was the Word, and the Word was with God, and the Word was God. He was in the beginning with God. All things came into being through him, and without him not one thing came into being. What has come into being in him was life, and the life was the light of all people. The light shines in the darkness, and the darkness did not overcome it."

Jesus himself said, "I am the light of the world. Whoever follows me will never walk in darkness but will have the light of life." John 8:12. The religious people around him did not believe. They accused him of lying about himself. They railed against him as a blasphemer. But to those who believed he gave the power to receive eternal life. They began to live the kind of life that is to be found only in relationship to God. They began to reflect the light that emanated from the very heart and throne of God into the world around them. So Jesus said to them, "You are the light of the world."

What an astounding progression we see here. From Bible promises, to prophetic fulfillment, to revealed embodiment of God in the world, to the transfer to us: The Light of the world turns in our direction and says, "You are the light of the world." It must have raised a thousand goose bumps on those disciples. It ought to raise a bunch on us as well. How does it feel to begin to realize that you are the light of the world? Those aren't my words. Those are the words of Jesus. Most of us, when we first hear them, say, "Who me?" We're akin to Mary when Gabriel appeared and said, "Greetings favored one! The Lord is with you." "But she was much perplexed by his words and pondered what sort of greeting this might be." Luke 1:28-29.

When Jesus says to us, "You are the light of the world," what sort of approbation is this? What's involved? What's the catch? What kinds of expectations are attached to being the light of the world? We are well accustomed to dismissing people who think "they are all that," people who are stuck on themselves, people who think more highly of themselves as they ought to think, people who are proud and arrogant. We snipe, "Who do they think they are, God's gift to the planet earth?"

It would seem that being the light of the world, if that's what we are, comes with some danger. First, we might become victims of our own pride. Second, we might become targets for the misunderstanding of our fellow human beings. We may become targets for jealously and resentment if we do this the wrong way.

Jesus comes immediately to our aid. The first thing he says after he calls us the light of the world is: "A city built on a hill cannot be hid." Now you might be a lot of things in and of yourself, but I can boldly assure you, you are not a city! Cities are populated by a whole collection of people. You can't be the light of the world all by your lonesome. The light of the world is going to shine most brightly through a group of people. We call that the Church. Our praying connects us one to another. So, does our worship. So, do our sacraments. Even when we are in deep solitude, we have been grafted into the Body of Christ. God enhances us to be unique individuals but our worth as individuals is only fully disclosed in fellowship. We share and receive gifts of the Holy Spirit in communion with one another. The whole New Testament is saturated with "one-anothering."

The Church of Jesus Christ is his building project. We seek a city whose builder and maker is God is how the writer to the Hebrews put it. Jesus's disciples together begin to exhibit a new kind of city on earth. It is a city that honors the government of God and begins to embody the character of God. It is a city that is no stranger to love, mercy, grace, forgiveness, and the willingness to endure even the opposition of enemies and the injustice hurled its way by those who have yet to see. Those yet to be reborn meet this city's appearance with hostility and suspicion.

In an instant, Jesus abruptly switches the image to that of a lamp. The whole purpose of lighting a lamp is to shed light in a dark place. He says no one lights a lamp only to cover it up or hide it. In a hostile environment, the temptation to hide our unwelcome light is strong. Being the light of the world can be dangerous in a world that loves darkness rather than light. But hidden light is useless, even ridiculous. Light exists to give itself away. It doesn't matter if it is particle or wave. Its purpose is to enable sight.

Jesus ties light to our good works that shine before others in such a way that it causes people to give glory to our Father in heaven. I remember long ago in one of my first brushes with science being in a class where a prism was brought forth. How magical it was to see bright white light refracted into all the colors of the rainbow. God's light shining through us is like that. You might come through as blue and I might come through as red, but together we are all included in the one light emanating from its source in God. Your works might be principally deeds of generosity, mine of mercy. Others around us supply other gifts in the working of God. And we know it is working best when people know that something bigger than us has been at work. We are conduits for a larger source. We don't want or need credit. We are delighted when people see through us and see God at work. And when they give God the glory, the circle of love and life closes in completeness.

Finally, there's one more precious gift wrapped up in this package of verses. Notice that Jesus says that glory will be given "to your Father in heaven." It was scandalous enough in that day that Jesus called God his father, even using that oh so familiar name "Abba" to refer to God, to the Holy God whose very name dare not be uttered by unworthy human lips. Now we see for the first time, Jesus giving his privilege away, placing the word "Father" upon our lips. When the disciples came to Jesus and said, "Lord, teach us to pray," he said, "When you pray say this: Our Father who art in heaven, hallowed be thy name." We've said that by rote for most of our lives with no inkling of just how radical and revolutionary that prayer permission really was the day it was given.

So here we are. We are the light of the world. We have the honor by how we live to reveal God to a world that can't see God. Our works don't save us. Jesus has done that already. Neither you nor I can add one single, solitary mote or mite to Jesus' accomplished work. When he said, "It is finished," he didn't mean "It's almost complete." He meant salvation is perfectly accomplished. It lacks nothing at all. The only thing left is for all men and women to see it. And now I will use my built city, the Church, and my Spirit filled people, my lamps, to reveal to the world the glory and honor due to my Father and their Father.

So now, citizens of God's city and lamps lit by God himself and placed upon a stand where you can be seen, uncover yourself. Then clothe yourself in humility and commit yourself to servant hood. When you do, people will be able to look through your life as it were a magnifying glass through which they will see God. And seeing God, they will give the glory that is God's due.

Strange Inheritance

I've never actually watched the show, but I've seen the ads. Fox Business has a new offering called Strange Inheritance hosted by an attractive blond lady who goes afield to find stories of people who inherit treasures that no one thought had any value for a long time. Then the discovery was made. That old nickel is worth one million dollars. Those baseball cards, originals and signed by players from long ago are worth millions. That vase, those toy trains, that.... well, you get the point. It's Fox's version of Antiques Road Show I guess. I guess the appeal is that most of us like surprises [when they are good]. We like the thrill of discovering hidden value, of unearthing buried treasure, of getting something just thrown into life gratis, without any special labor on our part. It's why people play the lottery. It's why they keep on sending in their entries to Publisher's Clearing House sweepstakes. When Mary and I were kids, we were exploring the woods behind our house and found some old, bleached out cow bones. We knew that we had stumbled upon real dinosaur bones and the natural historians were going to give us a million dollars for our find. Still waiting-just sayin'. Call me.

Today we recall the day when Jesus took Peter, James, and John and went up the mountain to pray. Oh great; another prayer meeting. Suddenly Jesus, this very down-to-earth, ordinary looking man, began to shine like the sun. So did his clothing. The glory cloud of God's holy presence rolled in and enveloped the tiny band. Then two of the most venerated figures in Israel's long history as God's people, two people who most would say were long dead, I mean loooong dead, showed up and began to speak with Jesus about his departure, his Exodus if you will, which would begin in the holy city, Jerusalem.

What they said exactly we are not told. There was probably some worship and adoration going on. There was probably some strengthening and encouraging too. There was probably an as yet expectant gratitude for Jesus. He was about to fulfill all that was spoken of him by the Law, personified in Moses, and in the prophets, represented by Elijah. And then, like icing on this holy cake, there came the Father's voice out of the cloud of glory, "This is my beloved Son; listen to him!"

Try to imagine yourself in the skin of one of those three disciples. Sure they'd already witnessed miraculous deeds of power performed by Jesus. They'd seen healings and acts of deliverance from demonic forces. They'd seen Jesus take on all comers, every scribe and Pharisee who came at him to trick him, accuse him, and condemn him as a false Messiah, every one of them had been bested and turned back.

Here was a man who spoke and acted and lived his life as one who had authority. Jesus knew exactly who he was and what he had come to earth to do. He was authentic and unassailable by his adversaries. They'd witnessed all this with their own eyes. Always before, the wonders were things Jesus did. Now this! This is a new kind of revelation about who Jesus is. And it was awesome! I guess you just never know what might happen on a Thursday at noon or at 3:30 on a Tuesday afternoon, at least when you are following Jesus. Maybe we've under rated prayer meetings. Glory may break out at any moment.

Does anyone here still live your Christian life infected with such expectation? I'm guessing the honest answer is, "Not so much." We get caught up with the daily routines, so consumed with our chores and obligations and with fulfilling our responsibilities. Who really has time to go aside, to go up on the mountain to pray? We end up giving God a passing nod if we have any time and energy left over at the end of our long days, or perhaps, if we are really pietistic, we'll give him an hour [or so, in your case, being stuck with a windy preacher as you are—sorry] on a Sunday morning. Or maybe we can squeeze in five minutes in the morning to spend with our Lenten devotionals, you know, the one our pastor wrote. It's the least we could do. But what if holiness, if God Most Holy, would prefer more than the least we can do?

To return for a moment to that Transfiguration story, Peter, as Peter is wont to do, Peter, who represents a part of each of us, Peter jumps to the front of the class and begins to evaluate the situation: "It is good for us to be here. Let's pitch camp. I'll build some shelters. Let's just make ourselves comfortable in the glory. Let's forget all this talk about Exodus and arrest and torture and dying on the cross. What more do we need than what we have right here?" Moses, Elijah, the Law and the Prophets, plus a shimmering Messiah, what more do we need? Jesus' answer, given elsewhere to Peter for such desires would still be, "Get behind me Satan; you are not on my side here." Here the Father says simply, "This is my beloved Son; listen to him," which might be fairly translated I think as, "Shut up Peter. Please return to your seat and pay attention."

The Transfiguration might be viewed as the sudden discovery of buried treasure. It might be seen as the revelation of a strange inheritance. The disciples, just like so many of us in this very moment, had trouble seeing the glory in Christ's common humanity. They did not yet have the hymns that we have, hymns that sing, "In the cross of Christ I glory, towering o'er the wrecks of time." They hadn't yet learned to cling to the old rugged cross. They hadn't yet learned to take their stand beneath the cross of Jesus. Their inheritance was still stashed away in the attics of dim perception and levels of unbelief that beset us all at one time or another.

And it occurs to me that the Transfiguration is more than just a revelation for the disciples of the intrinsic glory of Jesus, though it certainly was that first and foremost. But might it also suggest to us that we who follow Christ have been granted a generous share, a full enough portion of the same glory to cause our lives to be transformed?

Paul wrote that we have this treasure, this glory, this indwelling Spirit, we have this treasure in earthen vessels, to show that the transcendent power belongs to God and not to us. Paul is not using that language to describe some super spiritual glory for apostles only. He is teaching about the normal Christian life. The same power that raised Jesus from the dead is the power at work in us who believe. It works from the very inside, there in the deepest places of the human heart.

William Paul Young, in his second novel, <u>The Crossroad</u>, tells the story of an arrogant, self-centered, and deeply heartbroken man [though he is in denial about this last part] who falls and sustains a serious injury. He is lying in a coma in the local hospital, hanging between life and death. While in his comatose state, he somehow travels to a strange land, to a place in between time and eternity, where he begins to encounter both the Lord and, ultimately, himself. He is housed in a shack on an estate of some sort that is barren and whose walls are in disrepair. There are caretakers who diligently uproot anything that would come to flower. To make a long story short, the estate is the condition of his soul. He has managed to take what was meant for glory and turn it into a ruin.

At the center of the estate, he finally comes upon what is described as a temple, dark and impenetrable. As it turns out, this is what he has constructed due to the death of a young son. His grief has turned to disappointment, disappointment has ripened into anger and bitterness, and out of all that mess a fortress has been built.

Sorrow and loss have become the defining core of his own heart and of his life, which has now been emptied of all color and beauty. Finally, his confrontation there leads him into the realms of healing. You'll have to read the book to find out more. The Cross Road: William Paul Young.

I'm telling you this not as a tease or as a book report. I bring it up because I know that many of you have such an inner temple, a hurt so deep, a betrayal so devastating, a sin so shame producing, a loss, a sorrow, a grief so gripping, that your treasure is locked away, the treasure in your earthen vessel buried under the dirt of living in the fallen world. And I have a word from the Lord for you this morning: Jesus is calling you out. Jesus is calling you to come up on the mountain with him. Jesus wants you to witness not only his transfiguration but to experience your own as well. You have a treasure in that earthen vessel you call you.

Kierkegaard illustrates the human condition of most of us as being like a man who inherits a beautiful three story home. In Denmark in his time, the ground floor was referred to as the basement. In his illustration, the basement is unremarkable. The glory of the house is in the upper levels. Up there it is truly luxurious and elegant. But, Kierkegaard says most people move into the basement and there they stay, content to live the spiritual life only superficially, to skim along the surface of life, never to discover their strange and wonderful inheritance that is theirs, is ours, yours and mine, through Christ Jesus. That's why Paul prayed constantly for his converts that they would come to know the immeasurable riches that belonged to them in Christ. And the same riches belong to us in Christ. So he prays that we would know the height and depth and length and breadth of the love of Christ that surpasses knowledge. Paul in prayer for us all finds himself stretching at the outer limits of human speech to express the glory that is yet to be revealed. It's as though he is saying "Listen. Pay attention.

Transfiguration happens!" Once you get a taste of this treasure called the Spirit filled life you'll never be satisfied with less.

Way back, on our tenth anniversary, back when I was trying hard to hone my skills in becoming the deeply romantic husband you see before you today, I decided to pull off something special. We lived in Avondale then, 40 miles south of Philly. I saw an ad in the paper for a new hotel in center city. It was called the Four Seasons and the descriptions were enticing. They were running a honeymoon special. You could get the penthouse suite and be served breakfast in your room the next morning, all for $110. It sounds funny now, but that was still a lot of money to me then. Today, the same deal would probably cost about $700! I took the plunge and booked it. It was to be a surprise. I arranged babysitting, bought everything Jean would need, [after careful study of what she would need], packed a suitcase, and said, "Come on. We're going out to dinner in the city." The rest, as they say, is history.

Here's the point. The Four Seasons was so unbelievably elegant that we were forever spoiled after that. Anywhere we stayed, we would turn to each other and say, "That was nice, but it wasn't the Four Seasons."

So here is my tease, my enticement, and my warning to you. Once you get even a glimpse of transfiguration, of the glory of being with Christ, of the sweet sound of his voice and the satisfying experience of walking in his will, you'll never be satisfied with less. You'll say, "That's nice, but it's not Jesus." Jesus is God's Son, the Beloved. Listen to him.

The Night Time Is the Right Time

Thirst is one of the most basic of human experiences. We are told that our bodies are 98% water. When that percentage drops even a little bit we are said to be de-hydrated. Dehydration can amplify your sickness. Dehydration can quickly kill you. We can live a long time without food but not without water.

In the developed world we take water pretty much for granted. I just read recently where parts of Kenya are experiencing severe drought threatening the food supply of many people. Conditions have become alarming and deadly. The article caught my eye because of our missionary interest in Kenya because of our personal involvement through Peris and her family, and Charlotte's leadership in fund raising for that land. It has been a rewarding partnership for us as a congregation.

Kenya is just one spot among many around the world where the absence of potable water and water to support food production is in critical condition. The people, the crops, and the lands of far too many are in jeopardy. Many Presbyterian missions as well as many others have rightly raised funds to dig wells and to educate populations in water management. Without water, people die.

Baby Israel had quite a relationship with water by the time they got out of Egypt and into the wilderness. Moses had struck the waters of the Nile with his staff and Egypt's lifeline against the desert had turned into blood. After the Hebrews were released by Pharaoh to take leave of their life of slavery, Pharaoh changed his mind and chased them as far as the Red Sea. The waters stood like a wall against their flight until God opened the sea before Israel and they went through as on dry land to the other side. Then God used the waters to swallow up Israel's oppressors for good. The waters were used for deliverance and for salvation.

Hungry and thirsty Israel arrived at an oasis called Marah which got its name because the waters there were bitter and undrinkable. Marah means bitter. The people complained bitterly, their souls becoming a reflection of the water. Then God directed Moses to toss a certain tree into the spring which turned the waters sweet. But Israel, though temporarily satisfied did not turn sweet. Instead, very early on, Israel was learning as does just about every child that throwing tantrums was a way to get what they wanted, even from God, or so they thought.

A few weeks ago, my youngest granddaughter Keira was at my house early. I had yet to leave for work and I had my pocket calendar and my pen in my shirt pocket. She thought she deserved to put them in her mouth like she does just about everything at this oral stage of development. She reached for them and I thwarted her by covering them with my hand. We did this dance step repeatedly until I took her right hand in mine and held it. Her left hand shot out toward the desired prize but I blocked that move too. Then she turned away from me and sitting on the floor next to me commenced to produce a very dramatic fake cry and threw an angry little tantrum. I just laughed and easily diverted her attention to something else. She wasn't thirsty, just ornery. When you are thirsty you are not so easily distracted.

Israel stayed at Marah for a while, but their travels were far from over. No one confused a desert oasis with the promise of a land flowing with milk and honey. Refreshed, they pulled up stakes and traveled on. They got hungry. They threw a tantrum. God gave them bread from heaven, manna. All they had to do was collect it. They soon got sick of heavenly bread. They wanted meat. God

A Fellowship of Cracked Pots

gave them quails which they ate until it felt like it was coming out of their noses. More complaining ensued.

Then they got thirsty again and there was no water in sight. They threw a tantrum against Moses and against God. "Is the Lord among us or not?" was the question. Even after all the signs and wonders that had gone before, they still wondered. They blamed Moses for not knowing what he was doing. And they still didn't trust God to stay with them. They still suspected God was a fair-weather deity who would abandon them when the going got rough, when night time fell. "Why did you bring us out here Moses, to die of thirst?" Slaves, who just yesterday were thirsting for freedom, today were free people thirsting for water and willing to go back to slavery to get it. But God was just getting started. Sooner or later we all discover that God does some of God's best and deepest work after dark. The night time is the right time. And we also learn that tantrums are tricky things. All of us at one time or another may be prone to throw a tantrum against God when we don't get what we want when we want it. We may come to believe that tantrums are a good way to influence God in our favor. We may even end up accusing God with our own question: "Is God with us or not?"

Israel's murmuring in the wilderness displeased the Lord, not to mention Moses, who found their whining about as attractive as we find the whining of our own children. How amazing that Jesus in his total identification with us even tasted this aspect of human existence when hanging on the cross he cried out, "My God, my God, why have you forsaken me?" In other words, "God are you with me or not?" He wasn't whining but he was asking one of the deepest of human questions.

God instructed Moses to go before the people with the same rod with which he had struck the Nile turning its waters into blood, and strike the rock that stood in that place. When he did, water gushed out and the people were once again saved and satisfied. The place was named Massah and Meribah, which means proof and contention. There the people put Moses and God to the test.

Scholars tell us that this event is pregnant with the foreshadowing of Christ. Paul says that Israel in the wilderness drank from a supernatural rock that was Christ and the striking of the rock by Moses with the rod filled with the authority of God represented centuries beforehand of the Lord Jesus smitten once for all. Moses used his rod to turn the Nile to blood; the blood of Jesus brought deliverance to us redeeming us from our slavery to sin and our lifelong bondage to the fear of death. And the waters that gushed from that rock so long ago represented the rivers of living water that Jesus promised would flow into and out through the redeemed lives of all who would come to him in saving belief.

In the other account of this event in Numbers 20 Moses struck the rock twice in angry pride and that was the reason he was prevented from entering the Promised Land. All the complaining had worn Moses out and he became petulant in his service of God. But God would not share his glory with anyone, not even Moses. The Christ would be struck once for all by the will of God even though the cross seemed to be no more than the malice of human beings. Nothing would need to be added to Jesus' one death to ensure salvation. His one life laid down would be sufficient for all in all times and places. There was to be no confusion on this point. Christ's death needs no supplementary work added to it. We get in on salvation by faith in his completed work on the cross.

In light of this, listen to a few verses from Romans 5 once again:

Therefore, since we are justified by faith, we have peace with God through our Lord Jesus Christ. Through him we have obtained access to this grace in which we stand, and we rejoice in our hope of sharing the glory of God. More than

A Fellowship of Cracked Pots

that, we rejoice in our sufferings, knowing that suffering produces endurance, and endurance produces character, and character produces hope, and hope does not disappoint us, because God's love has been poured into our hearts through the Holy Spirit which has been given to us.

Did you hear it? That text is a text for the night time. So often when we are in suffering, nothing is apparent but the darkness. We find ourselves saying in hard times, "This is a hopeless situation. I can see nothing good coming. We say God loves us but this hardship seems to call God's love into question." With the old time Israelites we complain, "Why did you bring me out into this wilderness, to die of thirst? Are you with me or not?"

The main reason suffering produces endurance is that we can find no way out. If we could escape suffering we would do it in a heartbeat. But sometimes there seems to be no route for escape. We stand like Israel on the shore of the Red Sea with our slave masters bearing down on us from behind, things like fear and anxiety and despair threatening to overwhelm us. So, we either cave in or we run or we stand firm in Christ and endure.

Paul points to an outcome that most of us only see in hindsight, after the suffering has passed. We find out that we've gained new strength of character. We learn some things through suffering that we learn nowhere else. We've learned trust in God. We've gained courage. We've learned that with God nothing is hopeless. And we base our hope on the knowledge that God loves us. And we know that God loves us because we become aware that we are in an intimate relationship with God, in fact, God's Spirit has been poured into our hearts and bears constant witness that we are loved.

You can tell how strong God's love for you is by noticing when you first noticed it and by grace believed. Paul says it happened while we were weak, while we were ungodly, while we were yet sinners, and while we were enemies of God; that's when Christ died for us. You might say that we were loved to life in the night time of our humanity, and the night time turned out to be the right time. When we had nothing but the worst of us to offer, we were reconciled by Jesus' death and saved by his life!

I must say I'm a little curious at how often lately the messages we are receiving are "come to Jesus" moments. It could be that some have come among us who have never given their hearts to Christ and the Holy Spirit doesn't want anyone to miss out on grace. And it could be that some one of us has forgotten that our salvation gets played out in three time frames, past, present, and future. I have been saved, once and for all; it is finished. And in the present I am being saved every moment by the sustaining love of Christ. And in the future, I will be saved for all eternity when I am brought at last to perfection in Christ's presence.

It may be that believing in our salvation in the present moment is the hardest place to believe of them all, because it is in the present moments of our everyday lives that we face all sorts of suffering and tests and trials, and it is there in that mix where we are most tempted to throw a tantrum and cry out, "God, are you with us or not?" The question is understandable. The affirmative answer requires faith. Lord, give us faith and hope, and most of all give us love. Here in the night time show us once again that it is the right time.

The Poor Man Has a Name

This is one troubling parable. How can we who are, compared to most of the population in the world, clothed in purple and fine linen and who feast sumptuously every day, identify with anyone else in the story but the rich man? Even the poorest among us worshipping here today are fabulously wealthy compared to many millions of people.

A tradition has developed in my family that every summer or early fall, we have a crab feast on our back deck. Going back to when my kids were little and we would hold them during our time at the Delaware beach town of Fenwick Island. Now our love of those spicy Old Bay seasoned crustaceans has passed on to the next generation. Our grandchildren are now just as crab greedy as the rest of us. Mark claims he was called by God to leave western Pa. and move to his church in Maryland, but I know it was the prospect of living smack dab in the middle of crab country that led him there!

There's a fish market in the heart of the Italian market in south Philly where crabs can be obtained. To get back to New Jersey, you have to drive past a favorite site where panhandlers work to gain the sympathies of the affluent motorists who stop for the light before getting across the Ben Franklin Bridge. Their tattered signs say things like, "Homeless, please help." "Hungry." They do look pretty desperate. You hear people say, "Don't give them anything. They are scam artists. They actually live in nice expensive homes in Society Hill. They'll only use the money to buy drugs."

My daughter said she hates to drive by them because she feels compelled to give them something. I've found myself feeling relieved when the light is green and I can zoom on by. When the light is red I've often just steeled myself to ignore them, eyes front, windows closed, doors locked.

We rich people don't know what to do about the poor. We rich people who confess Christ are even more vulnerable. At all the major cathedrals along the Camino, there were posted by the entryways women begging, eyes downcast, straw baskets with a few small coins being shaken to draw attention to them. "Alms for the poor; alms for the poor." In Egypt, amidst the gold and wealth of Pharaohs on down to the present-day affluence of the few, you can see people young and old scrounging through the garbage and camping out in cardboard boxes right on the streets of Cairo. The chasm between rich and poor has been with us from time immemorial.

This story of the rich man and Lazarus was not totally original to Jesus though he did give it added depth. Similar stories were told among many of the tribes of the ancient near East. The story was a vehicle for teaching morality, ethics, and wisdom, perhaps around Bedouin campfires before retiring for the night. And perhaps Jesus adapted it for his purposes precisely because it was familiar and most likely because no one could pretend they didn't know what it meant.

The story actually gathers up a central theme running throughout the Hebrew Scriptures, namely that God has a special concern for the poor and needy. And it matters to God how all of us treat them, the hungry, the homeless, the widow, and the orphan. Jesus did not accept the clever ways that the Pharisees and other religious elites had developed to dodge their God-given responsibility to be compassionate and merciful. They even developed a theology that said if you were poor or broken or suffering or victimized by some calamity or other it was because you had sinned and offended the Holy One. The story of the rich man and Lazarus undercuts all

A Fellowship of Cracked Pots

these notions. This parable serves as a warning that all such deviousness among those who say they love God comes to a very bad end indeed. Let's delve into a few of the details.

My dad used to urge me to learn everybody's name from the first time I'm introduced because, as he learned in the Dale Carnegie course he took, "How to win friends and influence people," there is no sweeter sound to anyone than the sound of their own name. You all know what a miserable failure I am at this. It takes me months to remember your name, and now at my age, I've known your name for years and sometimes struggle to recall it! Ouch!

In our story, notice first that the rich man has no name. He has fine clothing and great food, but who is he really? I've known some wealthy people and one thing I've noticed is that they often don't really know who their true friends are. People often just see them for what they have, then covet it, and then sidle up to them, acting like friends as a way to get something from them. The rich learn to be wary. True friends are hard to come by. Defenses need to be up. Vulnerability needs to be reduced to a minimum. A true friend is someone with whom you can be open and vulnerable, someone whom you can trust. True friends are rare for someone with something to lose. People may learn your name yet still only care about what you have and not about who you are.

So, we have a nameless rich man. He has defended himself against the needy man, who sits at his very gate. Every time he goes in or out, every time he goes anywhere, there he is. He must walk on by, pretending he doesn't see him. He's preserving his silver and gold, he's not sharing even the crumbs under his table of feasting, but he is totally unaware that he is paying a very dear price for all that avoidance, all that self-willed blindness.

Refusing to see the poor, he begins to lose sight of himself. He begins to be oblivious to the life of the Spirit. He develops the habit of absenting himself from the things that matter to God, not realizing finally that he is fashioning the shape of his own torment. To him, Lazarus has become invisible. He's seen him so often that he no longer even notices him. Lazarus has been merged into the way things are, just like all panhandlers in cities and towns everywhere. We don't really know how to help them so we just turn off our eyes and then our hearts harden a little every day.

The other main character is an abjectly poor human being, extremely hungry, covered with sores that have become drinking fountains for the unclean and miserable street curs that roam the town. But this man has a name. What's in a name?

I have a new granddaughter as you know. We play with her and say over and over, "Hi Kiera; and hi Kiki, our adopted nickname for the young princess." When I recently baptized here into our faith and family, my question of her mother was, "What is your child's name?" Even our life in Christ is accompanied by our name. Often in the Bible, someone who begins to deal with God receives a name change, signifying a change in character. Saul became Paul. Simon became Peter. Our name becomes a peg upon which we hang our identity.

"Who are you? What's your name?" "My name is Bill, what's yours?" The rich man doesn't say, "Hi, my name is rich, or well dressed, or so full I could burst." The poor man doesn't say, "Hi, my name is starving or sore covered or dog licked." No, if asked he would undoubtedly say, "My name is Lazarus." Just because no human cares enough to ask him his name, God knows his name. And God looks upon him with compassion, and God fashions for him a blessed eternity.

Sooner or later, we get around to asking the questions: "Why didn't God just send some manna or a Good Samaritan to make up for the rich man's negligence? Why didn't God just do a miracle of healing and take away his sores? Why not this and why not that? But this story is bigger than reasons and answers to unanswerable questions.

This story is a warning story about outcomes and against spiritual pretense. With anyone, rich or poor, there is always more going on than meets the eye. And there is more at stake too. Most of us spend way too much energy on the futile "why" questions. What we ought to be asking is, "In light of who we know God to be, how should we then live who claim to know him and believe in him?"

In the parable, both men die. Lazarus died and angels came and carried him to be with Abraham. The Jews took great pride in being descendants of Abraham. He was called the father of their faith. Abraham served as the emblem of their spiritual security. "We are children of Abraham. God is pleased with us for that fact alone."

Unfortunately, that belief tended to ripen over and over again into religious presumption and very erroneous theological explanations. "We can treat people the way we want because we are children of Abraham. We can condemn lawbreakers and ignore the poor who have obviously displeased God. They certainly displease us with their importunate demands for our care and comfort. Therefore, we are justified in explaining why they suffer as they do and why it is okay for us to ignore them. God obviously doesn't care enough to help them so why should we?"

The rich man died and was buried. No sweet chariot swung low to carry him home. He was placed in a hole in the ground and woke up in torment. The thirst was intense and the agony relentless. And isn't it interesting that as he cried out to Abraham for mercy, he requested that Lazarus be the one to deliver it. Why not just ask for water? Why would he attach his request to the one he'd ignored for all those years?

I'm guessing that the agony had restored his sight at last. Not only did he see Lazarus, he knew his name, he saw he was precious in God's sight, and he perhaps knew that what he really needed was Lazarus' forgiveness. He himself had been callous and cruel and now he needed help. But alas, it was too late. The chasm between rich and poor, between the haves and "have-nots," had widened to become an unbridgeable gap between the blessed and the damned.

Well this is just a story, right? It's just a little morality play? No, no, it's much more than that. Jesus is taking aim at all those, whether old time Pharisees or new time Presbyterians and Methodists and Catholics and Baptists, at whomever will listen that it is of great consequence when we say we believe one thing and then live as though we don't.

If we say we believe that God takes special care of the poor and the needy, what then is required of us who say this is our God? The Jews back then said they believed in Moses and the prophets, all of whom prophesied and preached about God's compassionate care for the poor and needy. But just like most humans in any age, we then set about ways to make it so as not be too expensive. Compassion often is inconvenient. Kindness often costs more than you ever thought it would. And real concern is born of ardent devotion to Jesus.

Remember the story of the sinful woman anointing Jesus' feet with precious ointment of great value. And remember the indignation of Judas the eventual betrayer of Jesus who complained, "Why this waste. That ointment could have been sold and the money given to the poor." Judas, under the guise of being more spiritual than thou while actually withholding his heart's devotion from Jesus as well as intending to pilfer the money for himself, was seen through by Jesus in an instant. And he replied, "The poor you always have with you, but you will not always have me."

I've been reading <u>The Art of Spiritual Direction</u>, by W. Paul Jones and he says in effect, "If you really love Jesus, sooner or later you'll end up loving and caring for the poor who lay right at your door." Jesus plain teaching is that we dare not ignore the opportunities God sends our way. And his prophetic implication at the very end of the passage is to take care that our hearts do not become so hardened that even the resurrection will fail to get our attention and spark our obedience to the mandates of mercy and compassion that are integral parts of the Gospel we say we believe.

www.ingramcontent.com/pod-product-compliance
Lightning Source LLC
Chambersburg PA
CBHW052137110526
44591CB00012B/1757